AUTOMATIC INCOME

How to Use the Power of Dividend Investing to Beat the Market and Generate Passive Income for Life

MATTHEW PAULSON

Automatic Income: How to Use the Power of Dividend Investing to Beat the Market and Generate Passive Income for Life

Published by American Consumer News, LLC.
First edition: January 2017
ISBN: 978-1539737667

Cover design: Rebecca McKeever
Editing: Jennifer Harshman (HarshmanServices.com)
Book Design: James Woosley (FreeAgentPress.com)
Printing: Amazon CreateSpace

TABLE OF CONTENTS

INTRODUCTION

PREPARING FOR A SECURE retirement just isn't as easy it was 30 years ago. Investment returns were much more consistent on a year-to-year basis than they are today. There was no deluge of complicated investment options to choose from. You could either invest in major public companies like AT&T and General Electric, or you could buy one of a handful of mutual funds that were available at the time. Social Security was in the black and you didn't have to worry about whether or not you would actually receive the benefits promised to you. You could work for a big employer and know that if you put in the work, you would have a secure job until the day you retired.

In the 80s and 90s, you could simply invest in an S&P 500 index fund and receive consistently good rates of return on your money. Between 1980 and 1999, there were only two years where the S&P 500 had a negative annual total return and they were both pullbacks of less than 5%. You could build up a nest egg inside of an IRA or a 401K plan and know that it would consistently grow by about 10% each year. You could withdraw 4% to 5% of your portfolio each year in retirement without eroding your portfolio value and even give yourself a raise every year in retirement to account for inflation.

Unfortunately, those days are gone. Between the crash of technology stocks in 2000, the 9/11 attacks in 2001 and the ongoing war on terrorism, the S&P 500 had three consecutive years of negative returns between 2000 and 2002. We had a couple of good years in the 2000s, but those returns evaporated when the S&P 500 lost 37% of its value in 2008 during the Great Recession. Major American corporations, like General Motors and Merrill Lynch, went bankrupt. Tax revenue fell sharply and the national debt doubled in just a few years. Interest rates fell to near zero and the government had to step in and provide an unprecedented economic stimulus to get the economy back on its feet.

We have had some good years since the Great Recession ended, but the promise of working for an employer for life and setting aside money in a 401K plan, then having a secure retirement has all but disappeared. Corporations are no longer loyal to their employees. Social Security is effectively insolvent. Financial experts are now telling us that we are going to have to work longer and live on just 3% of our investment portfolio during retirement.

We can no longer rely on the government or big corporations to take care of us during our retirement years. We can't simply throw money at the S&P and expect to receive consistently good returns over the long term. These strategies may have worked for people retiring 25 years ago, but people who are in their 20s, 30s, 40s and 50s need a new investing game plan that will offer them superior returns, consistent growth, and the opportunity for a secure retirement.

Enter Dividend Investing

What if I told you that there was an investment strategy that could provide you with a secure stream of lifetime cash flow? If there was an investment strategy that would allow you to live off of 4% to 6% of your portfolio each year without having to ever sell shares of stock or touch your principal, would you be interested? What if this strategy was less volatile than the S&P 500 and has historically offered higher returns than the S&P 500? What if the income stream generated by this portfolio actually grew by 5–10% each year? Would you be interested?

This investment strategy actually exists and it's not a super-secret hedge fund that's only available to the ultra-wealthy, a little-known strategy that will stop working as soon as everyone knows about it, or the next Ponzi scheme waiting to unravel. This strategy is quite simple and frankly, incredibly boring—but it actually works. This miracle investment strategy is investing in dividend stocks. While it might not seem like there's anything all that special about companies that pay dividends, the performance numbers will change your mind.

Standard and Poor's keeps track of a list of S&P 500 companies that have grown their dividend every year for at least 25 consecutive years, known as the S&P Dividend Aristocrats Index. This group of 52 companies includes household names like 3M, AT&T, Chevron, Coca-Cola, Exxon Mobil, McDonald's, Procter & Gamble and Wal-Mart. It would be natural to think that these long-established companies wouldn't grow as fast as the broader market, but actual investment returns tell a different story.

The Indexology blog recently published a chart comparing the performance of the S&P Dividend Aristocrats Index to the performance of the S&P 500 between 1990 and 2015. While investing in the S&P 500 resulted in cumulative returns of about 1,100% during this time frame, the S&P 500 Dividend Aristocrats Index had cumulative returns of more than 1,900%.

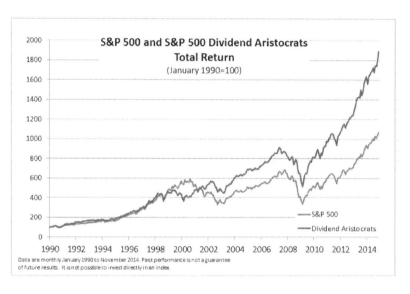

During the 10-year period ending in September 2016, the S&P Dividend Aristocrats has indexed an average annual rate of return of 10.14% while the S&P 500 Index has returned an average annualized rate of return of just 7.22%. No one will deny that dividend stocks have had a good run during the last few decades, but what about over the long term? It turns out that dividend payments are responsible for 40% of the annualized returns of the S&P 500 over the last 80 years.

Do I Have Your Attention Now?

Dividend investing really works and you can make it work for you, too. You can use the power of dividend investing in your personal 401K plan, your IRA, and your individual brokerage account to create an investment portfolio of dividend-growth stocks that will generate a steady income stream, be less volatile than the broader market, and offer returns that are superior to the S&P 500. You can build a dividend-stock portfolio that has an annualized yield of 4%–6% and that yield will grow by 5%–10% each year as companies raise their dividend over time. Dividend investing offers a perfect combination of income investing and growth investing. You get income from the dividend payments you receive as well as long-term capital gains from price appreciation in the stocks you invest in. If dividend stocks continue to perform as they have over the last 10 years, it's not unreasonable to expect an annualized rate of return of 10% in the years to come.

Just about everyone who is investing their money has the same goal— to have enough money in savings and investments so that you never have to work again (if you don't want to). You might want to retire at age 65 or you might want to retire early at age 55. Maybe you never want to retire, but you want the freedom and flexibility to work part-time or take a job you are passionate about that doesn't pay very well. Regardless of what your specific retirement goals are, dividend investing can help you achieve them. If you invest in dividend-growth stocks throughout your working lifetime, you can simply stop reinvesting your dividend payments at retirement and start living off the dividend payments you receive. You may never even have to sell any of the shares of stock you own, which will allow you to leave a significant inheritance for your children and your grandchildren.

How to Earn $100,000 (Or More) Per Year in Retirement

Let's imagine for a moment that you are 35 years old, are married, and have never saved a dime for retirement. You know that saving for retirement is important, but other things have just been a higher priority. You bought a house, you had a couple of kids, and you just never got around to opening a retirement account. You and your spouse decide it is time to take action and begin planning for your future and saving for retirement.

You and your spouse max out your Roth IRAs and invest $12,000 per year in dividend-growth stocks from age 35 through age 65. You don't have a 401K plan through work, you don't do any other investing, and you never increase the amount you're saving each year. You earn an average rate of return of 10% per year and reinvest your dividends along the way. At age 65, you would have a total $2.26 million in your retirement account. If your portfolio were to have a dividend yield of 4.5%, you would receive $101,700 in dividend payments each year.

By simply maxing out your Roth IRAs and investing in dividend stocks for part of your working lifetime, you can have a retirement portfolio that will generate $100,000 per year in dividends. You won't have to sell a single share of stock during retirement to pay for your lifestyle. You won't have to take a part-time job as a greeter at Wal-Mart, and you won't have to rely on the government paying you the Social Security payments you've been promised. Unlike most Americans, who retire broke, you'll have a steady stream of cash deposits coming into your brokerage account each month from great American companies like Johnson & Johnson, Coca-Cola, General Electric, Verizon, Wal-Mart, and Wells Fargo.

I Love Dividend Investing

In my role as the founder of MarketBeat.com, a financial-news service that makes real-time financial information available to investors at all levels, I have been looking for an investment strategy for the last six years that I could wholeheartedly recommend to the 425,000 people who subscribe to our daily newsletter. I evaluated the performance of just about every tried-and-true investment strategy and every hot new asset allocation only. Almost without exception, every portfolio I looked at offered unremarkable returns, would only work well in certain market conditions, or simply couldn't stand the test of time.

The only investment strategy I have found that has historically offered superior returns and has stood the test of time is dividend-growth investing, which is the strategy I use in my own personal investment portfolio. My portfolio currently contains 30 dividend-growth stocks and a few other income-generating investments. My brokerage account currently has a dividend yield of 4.45% and the companies I invest in have raised their dividends by an average of 7.3% over the last several years. If my portfolio companies continue to raise their dividends at their current rate, I'll be receiving a 9% dividend yield on my original investment after 10 years and an 18.2% dividend yield on my original investment after 20 years. My portfolio also happens to be 30% less volatile than the S&P 500 (as measured by beta) and has outperformed the S&P 500 since I started tracking my personal performance about three years ago.

I know what you're thinking: "Just tell me what companies you bought!" I have provided a list of ticker symbols for the companies I own in one of the appendixes for full disclosure purposes, but that does not mean you should just go and buy those stocks. The purpose of this book is not to recommend any specific dividend stocks or suggest the companies that I currently own are superior to the broader market or will offer above-average returns in the years to come. Don't just blindly copy someone else's portfolio. The way to do well with dividend investing is to do your own research, understand the characteristics of high-quality dividend stocks, and build a portfolio of solid dividend-growth companies.

What You'll Learn

This book is designed to be a primer for anyone looking to learn about dividend investing. It assumes you have a basic understanding of what stocks are and how the stock market works, but is very accessible to anyone who's just getting started. Here's what you'll learn in this book:

- **The Case for Dividend Investing (Chapter 1)** – You'll learn why investing in dividend stocks is arguably the best way to invest in the stock market. You'll learn how investing in dividend stocks compares to investing in broad-market indexes. You'll learn about how risky dividend stocks are relative to other investments.

- **Dividend Investing Basics (Chapter 2)** – You'll learn all of the terminology relevant to dividend investors. You'll learn how announcement dates, ex-dividend dates, record dates, and payable dates work. You'll learn about common types of dividend stocks, such as blue chips, real-estate investment trusts, utilities, master limited partnerships, royalty trusts, and business-development companies.

- **Evaluating Dividend Stocks (Chapter 3)** – You'll learn to tell high-quality dividend stocks from the rest of the pack. You'll learn why you shouldn't always invest in the highest-yielding companies. You'll learn how to evaluate the stability of a company's dividend and its possibilities for long-term growth. We'll also go through and analyze several stocks so that you can put your newly found research skills into practice.

- **How to Discover Great Dividend Stocks (Chapter 4)** – You'll learn what websites, newsletters, and research tools I use personally to identify, research, and evaluate dividend stocks. You'll learn more about the S&P Dividend Aristocrats Index and other lists of stocks with long track records of dividend growth. You'll also learn several shortcuts to identify companies that pay great dividends and have strong long-term growth potential.

- **Tax Implications of Dividend Investing (Chapter 5)** – Not all dividend payments receive equal tax treatment. You'll learn which types of companies' dividends will be taxed at capital-gains rates and which will be taxed at your ordinary income rates. You'll also learn how to invest in dividend stocks inside of a retirement account.

- **How to Build a Dividend Stock Portfolio (Chapter 6)** – We'll put everything together in this chapter and show you how to build your very own investment portfolio of dividend stocks. You'll learn whether you should invest in a dividend-growth mutual fund or ETF or whether you should buy individual dividend stocks. You'll learn if you should reinvest your dividends or if you should ever sell any of your dividend stocks. You'll also learn how to actually start living off your dividend stock portfolio in retirement.

Of course, I don't expect that this will be the only book on dividends that you ever read. In Appendix One, I've included a number of books, newsletters, and websites that you can read to learn more about dividend investing. In Appendix Two, I've included a list of the companies on the S&P Dividend Aristo-crats Index so that you have a starting point for your research. Appendix Three contains a legal disclaimer and disclosure of the dividend stocks that are currently in my portfolio.

Let's Get Started

The best time to start building your portfolio of divi-dend-growth companies was five years ago, but the second best time is today. It's never too early or too late to start investing.

Every month that you let go by without saving for retirement is a month of missed dividend payments and missed capital appreciation.

Make a decision today that you are going to take control of your future and begin building your investment portfolio of divi-dend-growth stocks.

Take the first step toward planning a more secure retirement by reading the remainder of this book and learning how to evaluate and invest in dividend stocks.

CHAPTER ONE

The Case for Dividend Investing

BEFORE DIVING INTO THE fine details of dividend investing, it's worth taking a step back and thinking about what goals you are actually trying to accomplish through investing and how you might best achieve those goals. If you're like most people, you're dependent on the month-to-month income provided by your day job or your business. If you were to lose your job or if your business were to fail, you would be in a world of hurt after a few months. The goal is to set aside money for the future inside of IRAs and 401K plans so that you don't have to continue to earn a paycheck in retirement. If you build a big-enough nest egg, you can live entirely off the money generated by investments and won't have to work a part-time job to supplement your income in retirement.

The concept of putting money away to live on during retirement is pretty basic, but most people are miserable failures when it comes to saving retirement. Thirty-three percent of Americans have literally nothing saved for retirement, according to a study from GoBankingRates. Sixty-six percent of all Americans have less than $50,000 set aside for retirement, which will cover 1–2 years of retirement at most. Only 13% of Americans have set aside $300,000 or more for retirement. If you are part of the vast majority of Americans that aren't saving enough for retirement, get ready to work a part-time job and eat beans and rice in retirement. Instead of playing with your grandchildren, taking life easily, and traveling around the world, you'll be stuck stocking shelves in a grocery store or greeting people as they come into Wal-Mart. If that's you, I implore you to start investing today so that you can have a better future in retirement.

Dividend Stocks Work Great for Retirement Investing

After you open up an IRA or set up a 401K plan through your employer, you have to decide what kind of investments you want to put your money into. If you're younger, the standard advice is to put money away into growth stocks that have a good chance to appreciate over time as you get closer to retirement. You will probably do okay owning growth stocks throughout your working years, but they are non-ideal investments if you're in retirement because you have to sell shares of the stocks or mutual funds you own to provide for your life-style. This might work okay when the market is doing well, but selling shares in a declining market will magnify the impacts of market losses. If the market declines by 2% in a year, you have to sell shares that were worth $62,500 a year ago to get $50,000 in cash. This effect, known as reverse dollar-cost averaging, means the market will need a significantly stronger recovery to get you back to your original account balance. For example, if the market were to decline by 20% per year and you withdraw 4% of your money in a year, you will actually need a 31.6% recovery to get back to your original portfolio balance.

For people getting ready to retire, the standard advice is to purchase lower-risk, income-generating investments such as municipal bonds, corporate bonds, and treasury bills. These investments provide stability and the type of steady income stream that retirees are looking for, but they just aren't able to generate the yields retirees need in the current protracted low-interest rate environment. As I write this chapter, a 10-year Treasury bill pays a yield of just 1.7%. The iShares National Municipal Bond Fund, the largest municipal bond fund, currently pays a dividend yield of just 2.26%. Since most retirees are looking to be able to safely live on at least 4% of their retirement portfolio each year, traditional income investments just aren't going to cut it until the prevailing interest rates rise to more historical levels.

Dividend stocks offer the perfect mix of growth investing and income investing. You can build a portfolio of dividend stocks that offers immediate income in the form of dividend payments and long-term capital appreciation as the prices of your stocks rise over time. You can easily build a portfolio of dividend stocks that offer a yield by 4% and 5% in today's environment, which will enable you to meet the target 4% withdrawal rate in retirement. You will also never have to sell any shares of the stocks that you own, because 100% of your withdrawals will be funded by the dividend payments that you receive. Since you're never actually selling any of your shares, you won't get hammered by the effects of reverse dollar-cost averaging in the event of a market dip.

Dividend stocks offer true passive income. You receive checks in the mail (or deposits in your brokerage account) every month or every quarter for simply owning a publicly traded company. You don't have to do anything other than continue to hold on to your stocks. Because companies regularly raise their dividends, the passive income you receive in the form of dividend payments will almost certainly grow over time. There is also no guessing about how much money you can or cannot safely take out of your account, because you can immediately know how much income you can live off of by adding up the amount of dividend payments you expect to receive over the course of the year. Dividend investing isn't without risk, but the combination of capital appreciation and income they offer make them very attractive investments for retirement.

Dividend Stocks Have Lower Volatility

Investors use a metric known as beta to determine the volatility, or systematic risk, of any given company relative to the market as a whole. Beta identifies the tendency of a company's returns and price swings to track with the broader market. The S&P 500 has a beta of 1.0. Companies that move with the market will also have a beta of 1.0. Companies that have a beta of less than one are theoretically less volatile than the broader market. Securities that have a beta of greater than one are more volatile than the market as a whole. Most technology stocks have a beta higher than one because they are higher-risk and higher-growth investments. On the other hand, companies in more stable sectors, such as utilities and consumer staples, will generally have betas of less than one. For example, iShares U.S. Utilities ETF has a beta of just 0.08. That means for every $1.00 price swing in the S&P 500, the iShares U.S. Utilities ETF will move about 8 cents.

As you might expect, dividend stocks are collectively less volatile and have less systematic risk than the broader market.

Most companies that pay dividends and continue to grow them over time are well established large-cap companies that have long histories of earnings growth. They have more predictable earnings and tend to weather uncertain times better. During market dips, dividend stocks generally don't fall nearly as much as younger, high-growth companies do. For example, the Pro-Shares S&P 500 Dividend Aristocrats ETF (NOBL), which tracks the S&P Dividend Aristocrats Index, has a beta of 0.77. If you were to own all of the companies in the S&P Dividend Aristocrats, your portfolio would be 23% less volatile than the S&P 500.

Having a portfolio with lower volatility won't give you better returns, but it will help you sleep better at night. Many investors make the mistake of selling when the market is in decline to avoid further losses and only get back into the market after it's already significantly appreciated in value. By owning stocks that don't jump around as much, you'll have much less of a temptation to sell out your positions when there's a market decline.

The Psychological Advantage of Dividend Investing

Dividend stocks have another psychological advantage as well. In lieu of worrying about the day-to-day value of your portfolio, focus on the perpetually growing income stream you receive in the form of dividend payments. By changing the metric that you focus on from something that is very volatile to something that will generally move up and to the right, you will be much less tempted to sell your shares during a market decline. You really should be focusing on the amount of income generated by your portfolio anyway, because the amount of income your portfolio generates is really the metric that will matter in retirement.

In Warren Buffet's 2013 annual letter to Berkshire Hathaway shareholders, Buffet told a story about a 400-acre farm he purchased for his son in 1986. I won't repeat the story in its entirety, but Buffet used the example of his farm to provide a world-class commentary about why investors shouldn't focus on the wildly fluctuating valuations of stocks:

> ... If a moody fellow with a farm bordering my property yelled out a price every day to me at which he would either buy my farm or sell me his—and those prices varied widely over short periods of time depending on his mental state—how in the world could I be other than benefited by his erratic behavior? If his daily shout-out was ridiculously low, and I had some spare cash, I would buy his farm. If the number he yelled was absurdly high, I could either sell to him or just go on farming.

> Owners of stocks, however, too often let the capricious and often irrational behavior of their fellow owners cause them to behave irrationally as well. Because there is so much chatter about markets, the economy, interest rates, price behavior of stocks, etc., some investors believe it is important to listen to pundits—and, worse yet, important to consider acting upon their comments.

> Those people who can sit quietly for decades when they own a farm or apartment house too often become frenetic when they are exposed to a stream of stock quotations and accompanying commentators delivering an implied message of "Don't just sit there, do something." For these investors, liquidity is transformed from the unqualified benefit it should be to a curse.

> A "flash crash" or some other extreme market fluctuation can't hurt an investor any more than an erratic and

mouthy neighbor can hurt Buffet's farm investment. In-
deed, tumbling markets can be helpful to the true investor if he has cash available when prices get far out of
line with values. A climate of fear is your friend when
investing; a euphoric world is your enemy.

During the extraordinary financial panic that occurred
late in 2008, I never gave a thought to selling my farm
or New York real estate, even though a severe recession
was clearly brewing. And, if I had owned 100% of a solid
business with good long-term prospects, it would have
been foolish for me to even consider dumping it. So why
would I have sold my stocks that were small participa-
tions in wonderful businesses? True, any one of them
might eventually disappoint, but as a group they were
certain to do well. Could anyone really believe the earth
was going to swallow up the incredible productive assets
and unlimited human ingenuity existing in America?

(source: http://www.berkshirehathaway.com/letters/2013ltr.pdf)

Dividend Stocks Outperform the Market

J.P. Morgan Asset Management issued a report in 2013 that
analyzed how companies that pay dividends performed compared to companies that don't pay dividends over a 40-year period. From January 31st, 1972, to December 31st, 2012, companies
that paid no dividends had average annual returns of just 1.6%.
Companies that cut or eliminated their dividends had average
annual returns of -0.3%. On the other hand, companies that ini-
tiated or grew their dividends during that 40-year window saw
average annual returns of 9.5% (https://www.ny529advisor.com/
blobcontent/897/96/1323361441857_journey_spring_2013_
speaking_investments.pdf).

It shouldn't be much of a surprise that companies that pay and grow their dividends have outperformed that companies that don't, since 40% of returns of the S&P 500 over the last 80 years have come from dividend payments. Let's imagine that you invested $10,000 into an S&P 500 Index fund at its inception in 1926. If you had reinvested all of the dividend payments you received, your portfolio value would have grown by an average of 10.4% per year and would be worth $33,100,000 by the end of 2007. If you had not reinvested your dividends, your portfolio would have grown just 6.1% per year and would only be worth $1,200,000 at the end of 2007. During the 81-year period between 1926 and 2007, reinvested dividend income accounted for nearly 95% of the compound long-term return earned by companies in the S&P 500 (http://www.etf.com/publications/journalofindexes/joi-articles/3869-the-importance-of-investment-income.html).

If you need further proof that companies that pay strong dividends regularly outperform the market, you need not look further than the S&P 500 Dividend Aristocrats Index. This group of 52 S&P 500 companies that have raised their dividend every year for at least 25 years has dramatically outperformed other market indexes over the last decade. During the 10-year period ending in September 2016, the S&P 500 Index had an average annualized return of 11.68% with dividends reinvested. During the same period, Dividend Aristocrats Index returned an average annualized return of 16.17%. It's hard to understate how dramatically dividend-paying stocks have outperformed the broader market given that they have outperformed the S&P 500 by a whopping 4.5% every year.

You Can't Fake Dividend Payments

When publicly traded companies announce their earnings each quarter, the numbers presented are often largely a product of accounting and may not be truly representative of the company's actual financial health. Skilled accountants and unscrupulous executives can make a bad company's financial look healthy on paper. This is exactly what happened with Enron in the late 1990s. On paper, the company's financials looked great. Behind the scenes, the company was transferring its losses and debts to offshore corporations that weren't included in its financial statements. The company engaged in numerous sophisticated accounting transactions between various legal entities to eliminate unprofitable entities from its financials. Everything looked alright on paper and the company's stock price remained strong and it had a sterling credit rating, but it was a house of cards behind the scenes and eventually collapsed.

Accounting numbers can be manipulated, but you can't fake dividend payments. Either a dividend payment appears in a company's shareholders' brokerage accounts, or it doesn't. There are no accounting tricks that can make a dividend payment look stronger than it actually is and you know that the company at least has enough money to make its dividend payments. This isn't to say that dividend payments necessarily mean that a company has strong cash flow, because companies will occasionally borrow money to pay their dividend during cyclical downturns. For example, Chevron has been borrowing to maintain its dividend recently because of cyclically lower oil prices. However, major financial institutions would never lend Chevron the money to cover its dividend payments if they didn't believe that it would be able to repay those obligations in the years to come.

Dividend Payers Tend to Be Healthy Companies

Companies that pay strong dividends and steadily raise them over time tend to be very healthy and shareholder-friendly. One of the best signs of a company's overall health is having strong positive cash flow (having new money come into the company) and a company cannot pay dividends over a long period of time unless they have the cash flow to support their dividend.

Strong dividend payers also can't carelessly acquire companies or launch speculative growth projects nearly as easily other companies that have similar cash flow but don't pay dividends. They have to cherry-pick the growth opportunities that are most likely to create shareholder value with their artificially constrained retained earnings. Any company that can return more and more profit to its shareholders each year for decades must be doing something right.

Dividend Stocks Protect Against Inflation

Dividend-growth stocks offer a much better hedge against inflation than bonds and other fixed-income investments. Most bonds pay a fixed interest rate over the life of the bond, meaning the interest payment you receive is the same in the first month you own the bond as it is through its maturity (which could be more than a decade down the line).

During inflationary periods, each successive interest payment that you receive has less purchasing power than the last. Because the bonds you own will be lower than the prevailing interest rate, the value of your bonds will decline to match the bond market's current rates.

Dividend stocks won't be immune to the effects of inflation, but publicly traded companies can at least raise their prices to match inflation, which will then be reflected in its annual earnings and dividend payments.

According to data collected by Robert Shiller, dividends from the S&P 500 have grown at an annual rate of 4.12% between 1912 and 2005, while the consumer price index (a commonly accepted measure of inflation) has risen by 3.3% annually during the same period. As long as a company grows their dividend as fast as or faster than the rate of inflation, shareholders' dividend payments won't lose any purchasing power.

Risks of Investing in Dividend Stocks

There's a lot to like about dividend investing, but dividend stocks aren't without risk either. There are several investment risks associated with dividend stocks that you should be aware of and factor into your investment decisions:

- **Tax Policy Risk** – Currently dividends receive preferential tax treatment under the U.S. tax code. Qualified dividend payments are taxed at capital-gains rates, which are either 15% or 20% depending on your tax rate. It hasn't always been this way, though. As you'll learn in a later chapter, Congress has toyed with dividend-tax policy several times over the last decade. If Congress were to remove the preferential treatment that dividend payments receive, dividend stocks would be less attractive investments and would likely fall in price.

- **Interest Rate Risk** – Dividend yields are regularly compared to the interest rates offered by other fixed-income investments on a relative basis. When interest rates offered by risk-free dividend investments rise, dividend stocks become less attractive relative to their fixed-income counterparts. As interest rates rise, there will be natural outflows from dividend stocks that will lower their share price and drive up the yield of dividend stocks.

- **Risk of Price Volatility** – Dividend stocks have the same risks that any other publicly traded companies have. Their prices will fluctuate as market conditions change. While stocks generally perform well over the long term, investors must be prepared for years where their share prices decline significantly. If you can't stomach a 30% decline in the price of your dividend stocks in a year, dividend stocks might not be the investment for you.

- **Risk of Dividend Payment Cuts** – When a company faces economic hardship, its ability to generate cash flow and thus make dividend payments will be constrained. If a company doesn't have the cash flow to support its dividend over the long term, it will have to cut its dividend eventually. The share prices of companies that cut their dividends tend to take a significant beating in the market, so it's important to monitor the companies in your portfolio for clouds on the horizon. If the company's dividend appears unsustainable, you should try to get out before the company announces it will be cutting its dividend.

Wrap-Up

There are a lot of qualitative reasons to like investing in dividend stocks, but what really matters at the end of the day when comparing investment options is risk-adjusted after-tax performance. In other words, how much of a financial return am I going to get for the level of risk I am taking on after all taxes are paid? In this chapter, I have shown you how dividend stocks have handily outperformed the S&P 500 and other asset classes over the last few decades. I have also demonstrated how dividend stocks are less volatile and have lower systematic risk than other publicly traded companies. Dividend payments also receive preferential tax treatment under current U.S. tax law. While dividend stocks aren't without risk, the numbers demonstrate they are very attractive relative to other investments.

CHAPTER TWO

Dividend Investing Basics

LET'S IMAGINE FOR A moment that you have a friend named Michaela and that she is starting a new company that will offer customized IT solutions to other small business. Michaela needs some money to get her business off the ground. She approaches you and offers to sell you a 25% equity stake in the business in exchange for $50,000.00. You want to help out Michaela and think her business has merit and could generate significant profits, so you decide to take the deal and invest in her company. You are now a minority partner in an IT consulting business. You don't take home any profit for the first year, but Michaela's company starts to generate some meaningful profit during the second year.

Michaela decides that she doesn't need to keep all of the money in the business and declares a dividend at the end of the year. As a 25% owner in the business, you are entitled to receive 25% of the dividend that is paid out. Michaela mails you a check for your share of the company's dividend at the end of the year and continues to do so as long as the company makes money and you remain a shareholder of her company. This is dividend investing in action.

It's easy to think of stocks, dividends, and other financial concepts as abstract terms that have no relation to the real world, but owning shares of a publicly traded company isn't that different than investing in a friend's business.

If you were to buy shares of Coca-Cola, you would become a minority owner of that company. Your ownership interest is equal to whatever percentage of the outstanding shares that you own. You and the other shareholders of Coca-Cola vote to elect a board of directors, which is responsible for overseeing the affairs of the business each year at the company's annual meeting, either in person or online through proxy voting.

When Coca-Cola makes a profit, the board that you helped elect can decide what to do with the money at the end of each quarter. They can hold on to it as retained earnings. They can reinvest it into the business or they can decide to return it to their shareholders in the form of a dividend payment. When Coca-Cola's board of directors decides to distribute part of the company's profit in the form of a dividend, you are entitled to your share of the profit distribution as a part-owner in the company. On the date set, your dividend payment will be routed to the brokerage account where you own the stock, at which point you can reinvest the dividend payment to get more shares or spend the money however you like.

How Dividend Payouts Work

One might think that it would be easy to determine which shareholders are entitled to receive a dividend payment, but hundreds of millions of dollars in shares of every large-cap company are bought and sold every day and it's not always intuitive about who should receive a dividend payment. For example, if you owned shares of Coca-Cola and I bought them from you after a dividend was declared, but before it was paid out to shareholders, which one of us should receive the dividend? Obviously, this isn't the first time this question has been asked. There are a number of important dates to be aware of whenever a company announces a dividend:

- **Declaration Date** – The dividend declaration date is simply the date that a company's board of directors publicly announces an upcoming dividend. This date has no impact on who receives a dividend payment.

- **Ex-Dividend Date** – The ex-dividend date is the day on which any new shares that are bought or sold are no longer eligible to receive the next scheduled dividend. If you want to receive a company's next dividend payment, you must buy your shares prior to market close on the day before the ex-dividend date. Having an ex-dividend date a few weeks before a dividend is payable makes it easier for a company to reconcile which shareholders are eligible to receive a dividend payment.

- **Record Date** – Shareholders must properly record their ownership on or before the record date (or date of record) to receive a dividend payment. Shareholders who don't register their ownership by this date will not receive a dividend payment. In the United States and most other countries, registration is automatic and not something you need to worry about.

- **Payable Date** – This is the date when dividend payments will actually be mailed to shareholders or credited to their brokerage account.

A Note About "Dividend Capture" Strategies

Since the only date that matters when determining who receives a dividend payment is the person who owns it at the end of the ex-dividend date, one might think it would be easy to game the system by only buying shares of companies going ex-dividend the following day, holding them for 24 hours, then selling them to receive a dividend payment without actually having to hold on to the stock. You could then buy shares of new companies every day and capture as many dividend payments as there were trading days in a month. This "dividend capture" strategy sounds like a great idea in theory and there are people who have actually tried to teach it as an investment strategy, but it almost never works in practice.

When a company goes ex-dividend, its stock price will generally decrease by a dollar amount roughly equivalent to the amount of the dividend paid. Companies do not explicitly take any action to lower their share prices because buyers and sellers will automatically price in the lack of the upcoming dividend into the company's stock price. These natural adjustments prevent people from trying to game the dividend system and capture dividend payments without owning a stock for more than one day at a time. Dividend capture strategies are very difficult to time correctly, rarely ever work, and are not something that I would recommend that you try to pursue.

Why Companies Pay Dividends

Companies that are growing rapidly generally don't pay dividends, because they want to put most of their cash flow from earnings back into growing the company. Fast-growing companies may use earnings to start a new division, purchase new assets, buy out another company, or fund other growth projects. For this reason, many technology companies including Amazon and Alphabet (Google) don't pay dividends. Additionally, companies that are more established may not pay dividends if they believe that they can create more shareholder value by reinvesting their earnings than by paying a dividend. This is the reason why Warren Buffet's company, Bekrshire Hathaway, does not pay a dividend. On a side note, Berkshire Hathaway does invest in a variety of dividend-paying stocks, such as Coca-Cola, General Motors, IBM, and Wells Fargo.

Established companies with mature business models generally do not need to reinvest their earnings at the same rate that high-growth companies do. When a mature company finds itself with excess earnings, it may return a portion of those earnings to their shareholders in the form of a dividend. Many investors like the steady income that dividend-paying stocks offer and see dividend payments as a sign that the company is strong and that management believes the company will continue to have solid future cash flow. Mature companies will often pay dividends to attract new shareholders, to create greater demand for their stock, and to drive up the price of their stock.

Regular vs. Special Dividends

There are two general types of dividend payments. Regular payments are made on a set schedule, such as every month or every quarter. Most publicly traded companies will pay dividends every quarter, but some stocks, ETFs, and mutual funds will pay monthly. Some international companies only pay dividends once or twice per year. The amount of a regular dividend payment is generally pretty consistent from quarter to quarter, unless a company decides to raise or lower its dividend because of changes in earnings and cash flow. Almost all of the dividends that you receive will be regular dividend payments. Special dividends are one-time payments made to shareholders when a company finds itself with excess cash or disposes of an asset. For example, Microsoft issued a one-time special dividend of $3.00 per share in 2004 as a way to relieve its balance sheet of a large cash balance.

Types of Dividend Payments

Most dividend payments are provided to shareholders in the form of cash, but there are actually several different types of dividend payments.

Here are some of the different types of dividend payments that you may run into as an investor:

- **Cash Dividends** – These are by far the most common type of dividend and will account for the vast majority of the dividend payments you receive. Cash dividends are simply a transfer of your share of a company's earnings to your brokerage account in the form of cash.

- **Stock Dividends** – A stock dividend is the issuance of new shares of stock to existing shareholders without any consideration (payment) provided in exchange for the new shares. For example, if a company declared a 5% stock dividend and you owned 10,000 shares, you would receive 500 new shares of the company. While stock dividends increase the total number of outstanding shares of a company, they don't increase the value of the company. A company that has a market cap of $1 billion isn't suddenly worth $1.05 billion just because they issue a 5% stock dividend. Effectively, a stock dividend is a minor form of a stock split designed to increase the number of outstanding shares in the market.

- **Property Dividends** – Companies may issue non-monetary dividends to their shareholders. A property dividend could come in the form of shares of a subsidiary company or be physical assets such as inventories the company holds. For tax purposes, property dividends are recorded at the value of the assets provided to shareholders.

- **Scrip Dividends** – When a company does not have enough money to make its dividend payments, it may issue a scrip dividend, which is effectively a promissory note to pay shareholders a cash dividend at some date in the future.

- **Liquidating Dividends** – A liquidating dividend is a return of the capital that was originally contributed by shareholders. This type of dividend often occurs when a company is getting ready to shut down their business.

As a dividend-stock investor, almost all of the dividend payments you will receive will be simple cash dividends. It is also possible that you will receive a stock dividend if a company wants to increase the number of shares it has in the marketplace without doing a full-on stock split. You may receive a property dividend if a company is spinning out a subsidiary as an independent company. Scrip dividends and liquidating dividends are very rare and you are unlikely to receive them as a dividend-stock investor.

Types of Dividend Stocks

When we think of a dividend-paying stock, we generally think of established blue-chip companies such as Johnson &

Johnson and General Electric. There are actually many different types of dividend-paying publicly traded companies that operate in different industries, have different corporate structures, have different tax liabilities, and have other characteristics that you should be aware of. The next several sections of this chapter outline some of the major categories of dividend-paying stock that you might choose to invest in. The tax treatment for each of these types of stocks is discussed in a later chapter.

Consumer Staples

Companies that sell products that consumers use from day-to-day, such as beverages, household products, personal products, and tobacco are labeled as consumer staples. Proctor and Gamble (PG), Coca-Cola (KO), Philip Morris (PM), and Unilever (UN) are examples of consumer-staples companies. Consumer-staples companies sell products that are non-cyclical, meaning that consumers still generally need to buy their products during an economic downturn. As a result, these companies tend to have relatively consistent earnings and cash flow. These companies also tend to be very well established and have large market caps as a result of consolidation that has happened over the years, which makes them perfect candidates to pay dividends.

Banks

Many large banks were established dividend payers that offered yields between 3% and 5% before the Great Recession. When falling asset prices wreaked havoc on their balance sheets in 2008 and 2009, almost all of them had to dramatically cut their dividends. Since then, many of the large banks have slowly started raising their dividend payments again. Many are currently paying dividend yields between 1.5% and 3%. There are a few banks, most notably Wells Fargo, that are beginning to pay dividend yields that are consistently higher than the S&P 500. At this point, it's hard to say whether or not banks as an asset class will return to their former glory of being high-dividend payers.

Energy Companies

Large-cap energy companies, like British Petroleum (BP), Chevron (CVX), and ExxonMobil (XOM), have a history of paying strong dividends. When energy prices are low, as they have been in the last year, these stocks' share prices take a beating and their dividends rise. As I write this chapter, crude oil is hovering around $45.00 and major energy companies are paying dividend yields between 4% and 7%. When oil prices increase at some point in the future, oil producers' stock prices will rise in tandem and their dividend yields will decrease to their more historic range of 3% to 5%.

Master limited partnerships (MLPs) are a subset of energy companies that are structured as publicly traded limited partnerships. Investors who buy units (shares) of MLPs become limited partners in the business and the company is run by its general partners (the company's management). The MLP structure is used almost exclusively for energy and utility companies. MLPs have some unique tax advantages because of their corporate structure, which are explained in detail later on in this book. MLPs tend to own energy pipelines and terminals, which makes them less sensitive to energy prices than large-cap energy production companies are. MLPs tend to have strong and consistent cash flow, which allows them to pay above-average dividends. It is not uncommon for MLPs to have dividend yields between 5% and 8%. Examples of MLPs include Spectra Energy Partners (SEP), Magellan Midstream Partners (MMP), and Enterprise Products Partners (EPD).

Royalty Trusts

Royalty trusts, like master limited partnerships, invest in assets in the energy sector. Royalty trusts generate income from the production of natural resources like coal, oil, and natural gas. Royalty trusts have no actual employees or operations of their own. They are simply publicly traded financing vehicles that allow large energy production companies to lease natural resource assets. Royalty trusts are operated by banks, which manage their financial interests, take care of their paperwork, and make distributions to shareholders. Royalty trusts' cash flow and distributions can swing wildly as commodity prices and production levels change, which causes them to have very inconsistent earnings from one year to the next.

The largest royalty trust in the United States is the San Juan Basin Royalty Trust (SJT), which owns oil and natural gas resources in the San Juan Basin of northwestern New Mexico. It is operated by Burlington Resources, a privately held oil-exploration-and-production company. Burlington Resources pays production royalties to SJT, which are then paid to shareholders of SJT in the form of distributions. SJT is managed by Compass Bank, a subsidiary of BBVA.

Many royalty trusts pay very high dividend yields, often in excess of 10%. Royalty trusts also have some unique tax benefits, which are described in detail in Chapter 5. While royalty trusts pay high yields, remember that the distribution payments they make are tied directly to the underlying price of the commodity owned by the trust. A wild swing in energy prices could dramatically change the value of your investment in a royalty trust as well as the dollar amount of distributions you receive. Commodity prices can be very volatile, so prepare for a wild ride if you choose to invest in a royalty trust.

Utilities

Utilities companies tend to be very stable and predictable businesses that generate strong cash flow. Because consumers will always need water, electricity, natural gas, propane, and home heating oil to provide for their basic needs, utilities companies tend to weather economic downturns particularly well. Utilities also operate as franchises that give them the exclusive right to supply electricity, water, or natural gas to a particular area, which means they don't really have to worry about a competitive company coming in and eating their lunch. Utilities companies have huge infrastructure requirements and can use the same infrastructure for decades. It simply wouldn't be cost effective for a new company to come in and try to rebuild existing infrastructure from scratch.

Utilities tend to be heavily regulated because of the monopoly positions they hold. State agencies establish standardized rates that utilities can charge for electric, water, and natural gas to prevent the abuse of monopoly power. These rates generally allow a utility to cover its normal operating expenses plus a fixed percentage of profits on top of those operating expenses. The profit margin that is permitted to utilities companies will vary from state, but target returns on equity of 10% to 12% are common. A utilities company's profit will be determined primarily based on how much water, electricity, or natural gas they deliver to consumers. If the company is generating a higher profit margin than state regulators desire, the regulators can force a rate cut. Conversely, if costs come in much higher than expected, utilities businesses can ask state regulators for a rate hike to cover their increased costs.

From an investment perspective, utilities tend to have relatively stable share prices and have limited opportunity for long-term capital gains. Utilities also tend not to raise their dividend much faster than inflation and generally pay out 60% to 80% of their earnings in the form of a dividend. Although utilities offer limited long-term capital gains and dividend growth, they tend to offer very high dividend yields to attract investor dollars. Utilities companies currently pay dividend yields between 3% and 6%.

Examples of large utilities companies include Duke Energy Corp (DUK), National Grid Plc (NGG), Southern Co. (SO), American Electric Power (AEP), and Pacific Gas & Electric (PCG).

Real-Estate Investment Trusts

Real-estate investment trusts (REITs) are a special type of corporate entity used to own and operate income-producing commercial real estate, such as restaurants, hotels, malls, warehouses, and hospitals and other medical facilities. REITs can either be publicly traded on a stock exchange or privately held. Publicly traded REITs give individual investors the opportunity to invest in commercial real-estate projects while maintaining the liquidity of their investment, meaning they can sell their shares on public markets at any time. REITs are required by law to pay out 90% of their earnings as dividends to their shareholders, which means they tend to offer above-average dividend yields. REITs also have different tax treatment than most other types of dividend stocks, which is addressed in detail in a later chapter.

Publicly traded REITs can either be set up as property REITs (sometimes called equity REITs), where the REIT owns interest in commercial real estate; or as mortgage REITs, where the REIT owns mortgages on commercial real-estate projects. Property REITs and Mortgage REITs have very different investment characteristics. Property REITs primarily make money by leasing space to commercial tenants and distribute the rent payments they receive as distributions to shareholders. Property REITs generate very predictable income and can make steady dividend payments because their commercial tenants are often locked into multi-year leases with set payment schedules.

Mortgage REITs borrow money commercially and lend it out to commercial real-estate projects in the form of mortgages. Mortage REITs make their money on the spread between the interest rate at which they borrow money and the interest rate at which they lend money, which makes them very sensitive to changes in prevailing interest rates. Mortgage REITs tend to do well in declining-interest-rate environments where they lock in longer-term mortgages and can borrow money at increasingly affordable rates as prevailing interest rates lower. Conversely, they tend to do poorly when interest rates are rising and the spread between the rates at which they can borrow money and can loan money narrows.

Mortgage REITs tend to offer much higher interest rates than property REITs, but their share prices and dividend payments tend to be much more volatile than property REITs. Because of the volatility of mortgage REITs and the unpredictability of future dividend payments, many dividend investors avoid investing in mortgage REITs and focus exclusively on property REITs.

Examples of REITs include Public Storage (PSA), Welltower (HCN), Ventas (VTR), AvalonBay Companies (AVB), and Simon Property Group (SPG).

Preferred Stocks

Preferred stock is a special classification of stock ownership that has a higher-priority claim on a company's assets, earnings, and dividend payments than common stock does. If a company falls upon hard times, its preferred stock holders must be paid their dividends before common stockholders receive any dividend payments. Preferred stockholders generally receive higher dividend yields than common stockholders, but the dividend payments on preferred stock are fixed and will not grow over time. Preferred stocks are said to have features of both stocks and bonds, because they offer fixed-income payments and also offer some opportunity for capital appreciation. Preferred shares generally do not come with voting rights in the company that issues them.

Some preferred shares are callable, meaning that the issuer can buy them back after a set date for a pre-determined share price. If interest rates decline, a company may buy back its existing preferred stock and reissue a new series of preferred stock with a lower dividend yield to save money. If interest rates are rising, a company will be less likely to buy back its preferred shares because it is effectively borrowing money at a below-market interest rate. Other preferred shares may be converted to common stock on a set date or by a vote of the company's board, depending on the original terms specified for the preferred stock issue. Whether or not a conversion to common stock is profitable for preferred stock investors largely depends on the market price of the company's common stock.

Many investors are attracted to preferred stock because of their above-average yields and stable share prices, although it can be a lot of work to research individual preferred-stock issuances. In addition to evaluating the company's prospects, investors must also research the characteristics of the individual preferred-stock issue they are considering buying. For this reason, many preferred-stock investors buy preferred-stock mutual funds and ETFs and delegate the work of selecting individual preferred-stock issues to professional money managers.

Preferred-stock mutual funds and ETFs generally pay dividend yields between 5% and 8% in today's market.

For example, the iShares US Preferred Stock Fund (PFF) is a popular ETF that primarily invests in preferred-stock issuances offered by large financial institutions. It has a dividend yield that hovers between 5% and 6% and currently has a beta of just 0.29, which means its price is only about 30% as volatile as the broader market. It charges an expense ratio of 0.47%, which is in line with the fees charged by other preferred-stock ETFs.

Business Development Companies

Business development companies (BDCs) are a special type of corporate entity that was created in the 1980s to encourage the investment of publicly traded funds into private equity investments. BDCs invest growth capital into small and medium-sized businesses in exchange for equity position, much in the way that private equity funds and venture capital (VC) funds do. However, VC funds are typically only accessible to accredited investors who meet very high net worth or income requirements. BDCs are usually publicly traded, which allows anyone to buy shares of them without meeting the accredited investor status requirement.

Business development companies have very specific legal requirements under the Investment Company Act that they must follow. According to Wikipedia, the Investment Company Act "(a) limits how much debt a BDC may incur, (b) prohibits most affiliated transactions, (c) requires a code of ethics and a comprehensive compliance program, and (d) requires regulation by the Securities and Exchange Commission (SEC) and subject to regular examination, like all mutual funds and closed-end funds. BDCs are also required to file quarterly reports, annual reports, and proxy statements with the SEC."

Business development companies, just like real estate investment trusts, must distribute 90% of their income to shareholders, but most BDCs distribute as much as 98% of their earnings as distributions so that they can avoid taxation at the corporate level. Because of this profit-distribution requirement, BDCs tend to offer extremely high dividend yields that can range between 7% and 20%. Don't be mistaken, though. There is no free lunch here. BDCs are effectively the rocket fuel of the dividend-investing world. They can offer dividend yields that you can't find anywhere else, but they are also very volatile, have inconsistent dividend amounts and can blow up in your face if you're not careful. BDCs invest in privately held micro-cap companies and can have very wild price swings that make the great dividend payments you receive moot.

Many dividend investors, including myself, avoid investing in BDCs all together because of their wild volatility and inconsistent payout amounts. BDCs can be exciting to watch, but they simply don't fit the mold most income investors are looking for—established players that have consistent and growing dividend payments over time.

Wrap-Up

Some of the concepts and types of corporate structures in this chapter may be hard to remember at first. Fortunately for you, there's no quiz at the end of this book. Use this chapter as a reference guide to review dividend-investing concepts and how different corporate structures work when evaluating individual companies. Always be mindful of the types of corporate structures that companies that you invest in use, because each corporate structure has unique tax rules and investment characteristics.

CHAPTER THREE

How to Select Dividend Stocks

AS YOU BEGIN TO research dividend-paying stocks, you may be tempted to open your favorite stock screener, sort companies by their dividend, and focus on the companies that pay the highest dividend yields. Unfortunately, there is no such thing as a free lunch in the stock market. If a company is paying a dividend yield that is four or five times greater than the dividend yield of the S&P 500, there is a pretty strong chance that the dividend isn't going to stick around. Companies that offer dividend yields of 7% or greater may seem alluring, but these high yields are often the result of a significant drop in a company's share price and weak earnings that cannot support the company's dividend over the long term.

A while back, a friend of mine invested in The Williams Companies (WMB) when it was trading at around $22.00. The company's share price had taken a major hit and it was paying an annual dividend of $2.56, which works out to a yield of about 11.5%.

As a novice dividend investor, he purchased the stock purely based on the company's larger-than-average dividend. If he had done a little bit more research, he would have realized that the company only earned $0.84 cents per share in 2015 and there was no way that they could sustain their dividend. He received exactly two quarterly dividend payments at $0.64 each before the company announced it was cutting its annual dividend by 69% in the third quarter of 2016.

As an income investor, your goal is to get the best yield available on your money. This can make it very tempting to focus on dividend yield alone, but there are several other criteria that you should use to evaluate divided dividend stocks.

You want to make sure that the company will be able to continue to pay out its current dividend by looking at important financial metrics including a company's dividend payout ratio, debt, net margins, and return on equity.

You will also want to determine if your dividend is likely to grow in the future, as evidenced by the company's expected future earnings growth and its history of raising its dividend. You will also want to know whether or not you are paying a fair price for a dividend stock and are getting a historically competitive dividend yield.

Use the criteria outlined in this chapter to evaluate each potential dividend stock purchase and you will have a pretty good idea whether or not the companies you are buying will be able to maintain and grow their dividend over time.

Dividend Yield

Dividend yield is simply the measure of what percentage of a company's current share price is paid out in dividends each year. Let's imagine that there is a company called PretendCorp that has a share price of $100.00 and it pays an annual dividend of $2.50. PretendCorp's dividend yield is 2.5%.

A company's dividend yield will fluctuate throughout the day as the price of the company's stock rises and falls with the market. If a company's stock is doing exceptionally well, its dividend yield will fall as the stock's share price rises. If PretendCorp's share price were to rise to $150.00 and its dividend does not change at $2.50 per share, the company's dividend yield would fall to 1.67%. If a company is getting hammered in the market and its price drops, the company's dividend yield will rise. If PretendCorp were to post dismal earnings and its share price dropped to $50.00, its dividend yield would rise to 5.0%.

Focus on publicly traded companies that pay a dividend at least 50% higher than that of the S&P 500. As a stock investor who is looking for income, it only makes sense to focus on companies that pay a significantly higher yield than the broad-market indexes.

As I write this book, the S&P 500 offers a historically low dividend yield of 2.05%. That means the minimum dividend you should be looking for is 3.075% in today's environment. On the other hand, you should treat companies that pay an unusually high dividend yield with a healthy level of skepticism. If a company's dividend yield is more than three times greater than the dividend yield of the S&P 500, do extensive research about the company's commitment to its dividend and its ability to maintain its dividend before investing your money. In today's environment, that means you should evaluate a company that pays of 6.15% or higher with an extra amount of care and due diligence.

Companies that pay extremely high dividend yields often come with outsized investment risks and their dividend may be at risk of being cut, but that doesn't mean you should avoid dividend stocks with high yields entirely.

I personally focus my effort on companies that pay dividend yields between 3.5% and 6.5%. I consider this the "Goldilocks zone" or sweet spot of dividend yields. Companies that pay dividends in this range offer high-enough yields to pique our interest as dividend investors, but not so high that the dividend is unlikely to stay around in the future.

History of Dividend Growth

If a company you are evaluating has an attractive dividend yield, the next step is to look at the history of dividend payments. How many years in a row has the company raised its dividend? Has the company ever cut its dividend during a recession? How much does the company raise its dividend every year, on average?

Ultimately, we are looking for reliable dividend payments that are likely to steadily grow over time regardless of current market conditions. If a company has a track record of raising its dividend every year over the course of a couple of decades, there is a strong likelihood that it will continue along the same path of steadily raising its dividend if it is financially able to do so.

When I research a dividend stock, I pay special attention to what happened with the company's dividend in 2008 and 2009 during the Great Recession. During the six-month period between September 2008 and October 2009, 46 companies on the S&P 500 reduced or eliminated their quarterly dividend payments. During the same period, 82 S&P 500 companies were able to raise their dividend through the depths of the Great Recession. Granted, some of those increases were token bumps so that companies could boast about their track record of raising their dividends every year. If a company was able to maintain and grow its dividend throughout 2008 and 2009 while the global economy was in bad shape, that's a pretty good sign that the company is committed to its dividend and will be able to continue to making dividend payments during challenging economic times.

I personally focus on companies that have raised their dividend every year for at least the last 10 years. If a company has raised its dividend 10 years in a row, that is a pretty good indication that the company's management is committed to growing its annual dividend. You should also read what the company's management has to say about its dividend in its quarterly earnings reports and other public commentary to make sure that the company will continue to be committed to its dividend in the future. I also focus on companies that have grown their dividend by an average of 5% to 10% over the last three years. I am willing to accept lower dividend-growth rates on companies that have dividend yields on the higher end of the 3.5% to 6.5% spectrum I target. For companies that have a dividend yield of less than 4%, I will want to see an annual dividend-growth rate very close to 10%.

How fast your portfolio companies raise their income will have a huge impact on the dividend income created by your portfolio over time. Let's imagine that you owned a portfolio of dividend stocks that raise their dividend by an average of 7% each year. If you had a dividend portfolio that started out with a yield of 4.5%, you would be receiving dividend payments equal to 10.1% of your original investment after holding them for 12 years. After holding your investments for 25 years, you would be receiving dividend payments equal to 24.4% of your original investment each year.

> TIP: You can use MarketBeat.com to look up a company's annual dividend, its dividend yield, its dividend payout ratio, its forward-looking dividend payout ratio, its track record of consecutive years of dividend growth, its 3-year average of annual dividend growth, and other important financial metrics. Simply head on over to MarketBeat.com in your favorite web browser and enter the ticker symbol of the stock you are researching in the search box. When that stock's company profile page loads, click the "Dividends" tab to access these metrics.

Earnings Growth and Dividend Payout Ratio

A company's track record of steadily raising their dividend and its management's commitment to its dividend are always a good sign, but a company may be forced to reduce or eliminate its dividend if the company's earnings can no longer support its dividend. Dividends are paid to shareholders out of earnings. If a company's earnings are stagnant on a year-over-year basis, the company may not raise its dividend at all or it may merely issue a token dividend increase to maintain its track record of consecutively raising dividends every year. If a company's earnings decline for several quarters in a row and it must pay out an unsustainably high percentage of its earnings as dividends, its board of directors may be forced to reduce or eliminate its dividend.

The measure which shows what percentage of a company's earnings is being paid out as a dividend is known the dividend payout ratio. Dividend payout ratio is calculated by taking the company's annual dividend and dividing it by its earnings per share. For example, Wells Fargo currently pays out an annual dividend of $1.52 per share. The company has posted earnings per share of $4.08 per share over the last four quarters. This would put Wells Fargo's current dividend payout ratio at a healthy 37.2%.

You should also calculate a company's forward-looking dividend payout ratio by dividing an average of analysts' EPS estimates for the next fiscal year by its dividend. While a company may have a healthy dividend payout ratio now, you may be able to spot clouds on the horizon ahead if multiple analysts are forecasting a significant earnings decline in the coming quarters. If analysts were predicting that Wells Fargo's earnings were going to drop by 50% over the next year to $2.04 per share (they're not), its dividend payout ratio would rise to a much less healthy 74.5% and the continuation of its current dividend would be less of a sure thing.

The companies that you invest in as a dividend investor will generally have a relatively high dividend payout ratio. It only makes sense that companies that pay out strong dividends will pay out a significant portion of their earnings as dividends. Most of the companies that I personally invest in have dividend payout ratios between 40% and 70%. You should generally avoid companies that have a payout ratio higher than 75%, because there isn't a lot of money left over to reinvest in the growth of the business and a short-term earnings hiccup could force the company to cut its dividend. However, a very high payout ratio does not mean a company will automatically cut its dividend. Companies tend to be reluctant to cut their dividends and will sometimes borrow money or use retained earnings to pay their annual dividend during periods of weak earnings.

Real estate investment trusts (REITs), business development companies (BDCs), and master limited partnerships (MLPs) are the two exceptions to the suggested 75% dividend payout ratio limit. REITs and BDCs are required by law to pay out 90% of their income to shareholders in the form of dividend. Logically, REITs and BDCs will generally have dividend payout ratios that exceed 90% because of this rule. While MLPs do not have the same requirement to pay out 90% of their income as distributions, they tend to have strong cash flow but weak reported earnings due to the capital-intensive nature of their businesses. Consequently, MLPs generally have very high reported dividend-payout ratios.

When evaluating the sustainability of dividend payments for REITs and MLPs, calculate a company's payout ratio based on its distributable cash flow rather than its reported earnings. Distributable cash flow is a measure of profitability that identifies how much money the company actually has to use for paying out dividends, reducing debt, investing in growth, or buying back its own shares. Distributable cash flow can be calculated by taking cash flow from operations minus capital expenditures, preferred dividends, debt service, and other one-time items. By dividing a REIT or MLP's dividend per share into its distributed cash flow per share, you can calculate a ratio that will provide a better idea of the sustainability of the company's dividend.

Debt

Banks will rarely lend more money to people that are already deeply in debt, because they know that consumers that have a heavy debt burden are already paying out a large percentage of their income in debt payments and simply don't have the cash flow to make payments on new debt. Likewise, publicly traded companies that have a large amount of debt are often limited in their ability to return capital to shareholders in the form of dividends because much of their cash flow goes toward making debt payments.

You can determine a publicly traded company's debt burden by looking at its debt-to-equity ratio, which is simply the amount of debt the company has divided by the amount of shareholder equity. A debt-to-equity ratio of 1:1 is generally acceptable and any ratio lower than that is even better.

Debt-to-equity ratios will vary from industry to industry. In industries like telecommunications, manufacturing, and utilities, debt-to-equity ratios will be higher because companies in these industries use debt to finance long-term, large-scale projects. Companies in industries that have lower infrastructure requirements, such as consumer discretionary and consumer staples companies, will generally have lower debt-to-equity ratios. When evaluating a company's debt-to-equity ratio, make sure to compare it to the debt-to-equity ratios of other companies in the same industry so that you are making a true apples-to-apples comparison of how much debt a company has compared to its competitors.

Profitability

A good way to determine whether or not a company will continue to have free cash flow to pay its dividend is by looking at the company's net profit margins, which often gets shortened to "net margins." Net margin is a metric that calculates the percentage of a company's net revenue that is kept as profit. If a company has gross revenue of $1 billion and keeps $200 million as profit at the end of the year, it has a 20% net margin.

Companies that have higher net margins are able to weather economic turmoil easier than companies with lower net margins are able to because they can better temporarily weather periods of lower sales or higher expenses. For example, Buffalo Wild Wings (BWLD) has a net margin that hovers between 5% and 6%. If there was a major recession and the company had to lower the price of its menu items by 10% to attract new customers, the company would be losing money each quarter. BWLD competitor Dave and Busters (PLAY) currently has a net margin of about 12%. If it had to similarly discount its menu items by 10% for a period of time, it could still maintain its profitability. While neither BWLD nor PLAY currently pays a dividend, PLAY would be much better able to continue to pay a dividend during challenging economic times because it has higher profit margins than its competitor BWLD.

Profit margins will vary significantly from industry to industry, so there's no hard-and-fast rule indicating what would be considered a healthy net margin for any given dividend stock. However, you should demand minimum net margins of at least 5% in the companies that you invest in because net margins can vary depending on current economic conditions. By requiring a minimum level of profitability, you can avoid relying on getting dividend payments from companies whose ability to generate profit during challenging economic conditions is in question.

Another way to measure a company's profitability is return on equity (ROE), which can be calculated by dividing a company's net income by the company's shareholder equity. ROE shows the percentage of net income that a company is generating relative to the amount of money that shareholders have invested in the company. Companies that have a higher ROE percentage are more efficient in utilizing their shareholder equity to generate returns for their shareholders.

Generally speaking, analysts consider a 15–20% ROE percentage as good. ROE is particularly useful for comparing the profitability of multiple companies in the same industry. If you were considering investing in either Coke or Pepsi, you might compare their ROE percentages as a means of seeing which company is more profitable.

ROE is a metric that can fluctuate significantly from quarter to quarter, so a multi-year average ROE might be a better tool for comparison than simply looking at the data for the most recent quarter.

> TIP: You can easily look up a company's historical debt-to-equity ratios, net margins, and return-on-equity numbers using YCharts. com. The easiest way to find the specific metric you are looking for is to do a Google search of the YCharts.com website. For example, if you wanted to find Apple's net margins, you would do a Google search for "site:ycharts.com Apple net margins".

Fair Value Estimate

There is an inverse correlation between a company's share price and its dividend yield, which makes it especially important to pay attention to the ups and downs of the market and buy companies when they have been beat up a little bit, their share price is down, and their dividend yield is higher than usual. Some of the best buys that you will make as a dividend investor will occur when an otherwise good company's share price is getting hammered over short-term bad news, such as weak earnings or a major lawsuit.

Cummins (CMI), a major diesel engine manufacturer, saw its share price drop from $120.00 in September 2015, to a low of around $83.50 in January 2016 after seeing a year-over-year decline in revenue. I thought Cummins was fundamentally a good company, given that it makes a sizable portion of the world's diesel engines, and that the stock was oversold. I bought shares of the company at $86.37 and was able to lock in a yield of 4.75%. In the seven months that followed my purchase, the company's share price rose back up to around $125.00 and its dividend yield dropped down to 3.25%. Because I was fortunate enough to purchase the stock when its share price was depressed, I was able to lock in a yield much higher than Cummins investors are able to get today and had the added benefit of price appreciation in the shares I bought.

My favorite tool to determine where a company is trading relative to its intrinsic value is Morningstar's (www.morningstar.com) proprietary fair value estimates. Morningstar's analysts issue estimates of what they think any given stock should currently be priced at given the company's financials, long term prospects, economic moat, and other factors. Fair value estimates attempt to strip away the irrationality of the market and provide a general idea of what a stock should be priced at so that you know whether or not you are overpaying for a stock. Morningstar's fair value estimates are far from a perfect metric, because all equities research analysts are fallible, but they can provide a helpful idea whether or not a stock has been overbought or oversold.

You do need a Morningstar premium account or a subscription to Morningstar Dividend Investor to look up fair value estimates. Morningstar premium subscriptions are currently sold for $23.95 per month or $199.00 per year. More information about Morningstar's premium subscription offerings can be found at http://members.morningstar.com/.

Another way that you can determine whether or not a dividend stock is a currently a good buy is by looking at a chart of the company's dividend yield over time. By looking at a graphic representation of the company's annual dividend relative to its share price over a period of several years, you can easily see whether the company's dividend is currently higher or lower than its historical average. You can use the website Dividend.com to chart a company's dividend yield over time by entering in the name of any publicly traded company in their search box. On the Dividend.com's information page for the company you are searching for, scroll down to the section titled "Dividend Yield & Stock Price History" and click on the "Yield" link in the chart legend to view a chart of the company's dividend yield over time.

Using Dividend Discount Model to Develop a Fair Value Estimate

Dividend discount models (DDMs) attempt to identify a fair price for a stock based on the expected future dividends that shareholders will receive. DDMs generally assume that the only real value that stocks provide to shareholders is the dividend stream that the companies produce.

The theory is that capital gains and volatility in share price is the result of investors adjusting their expectations for a company's future stream of dividend income. DDMs attempt to project the value of all future dividends and then discount them to a net present value that identifies a fair value for the company's current share price. By using a DDM calculation, you can identify whether or not a company is currently trading above or below its intrinsic value.

Many investors use this simplified dividend discount model:

Expected Share Price = Annual Dividend /
(Cost of Equity – Dividend-Growth Rate)

This equation involves taking the company's annual dividend and dividing it by the cost of the company's equity minus the company's expected long-term growth rate. For example, Realty Income Corp (O) currently pays an annual dividend of $2.42 per year. If we use 10% as our cost of equity and expect Reality Income Corp's dividend to grow by 6% per year over the long term, the DDM above would suggest a fair price for the stock would be $60.50 ($2.42 / (.10 - .06)).

This simplified form of a dividend discount model can be helpful in identifying a fair price to pay for a stock, but we should be cautious about how much attention we pay to DDM calculations. The equation above assumes that the company's dividend-growth rate will never change and that the company's cost of equity will also never change.

We may also not have a good idea of what the company's cost of capital actually is and what the company's long-term average annual dividend-growth rate will be. Because this equation only uses three inputs, it is very easy to calculate, but the results of the equation are very sensitive to the numbers you use. For example, changing Realty Income Corp's long-term dividend-growth rate to 7% would raise its fair value to $80.67 (33% higher than the fair value calculated using a 6% long-term growth rate).

Economic Moats

In medieval times, a moat was a body of water that surrounded a castle in order to keep out potential invaders. In the modern era, an economic moat describes certain advantages that some companies have that allow them to stay ahead of the competition. The larger the moat a company has, the more likely that it will continue to be a profitable and viable business in the years to come.

There are several types of competitive advantages that can create an economic moat for a company:

- **Barriers to Entry** – Some industries have high financial or regulatory barriers to entry that would make it extremely difficult for new competitors to enter the market. For example, it would be almost impossible to create a new railroad network in the United States because of the thousands of tracts of land that would need to be bought from private-property owners. The four major players in the space (Union Pacific, BNSF, CSX, and Norfolk Southern) have huge economic moats simply because there are unlikely to be any new rail lines in the United States. In order to unseat the four major railways, an entirely new transportation method that is cost-competitive with rail would need to be invented.

- **Brand Name** – Consumers are naturally more likely to buy products and services from a brand that they are already familiar with than one that they have never heard of. Many companies have tried to make soft drinks that taste better than Coca-Cola, but none has been able to unseat Coca-Cola as the world's dominant soft-drink producer because the Coca-Cola brand is so ingrained in the minds of consumers. Having a strong brand name also allows Coca-Cola to maintain pricing power over its competitors. You can buy a can of generic cola for $0.25 in a grocery store, but you are two to three times more likely to get the brand of soft drink that you are familiar with and already know you enjoy.

- **Economies of Scale** – Companies that produce, transport, and sell goods at larger scale than their competitors can often benefit from reduced costs that their competitor can't match. Wal-Mart (WMT) is the perfect example of a company that benefits from having economies of scale. Because they have more than 4,000 stores in the United States and sell nearly $500 billion per year in annual revenue, they can purchase goods from suppliers more cheaply than their smaller competitors can. This allows them to sell goods at lower prices while earning higher profit margins than smaller competitors do.

- **High Switching Costs** – If it takes a significant amount of time, money, or effort for a customer to switch from one company or another, customers are much less likely to move their business elsewhere. High switching costs insulate an existing company from upstart competitors because it will be difficult for the new company to steal the existing company's customers. For example, people rarely switch banks because it takes a lot of work to set up new accounts, update their direct-deposit records, change payment methods for recurring subscriptions, and move their money over. Even if you're unhappy with your current bank, it's just easier to stay where you are because of the amount of work involved with switching to another bank.

- **Other Intangible Assets** – Some companies benefit from patents and trademarks that prevent companies from making similar or identical products. For example, prescription-drug companies that patent a new medicine will receive the right to be the exclusive seller of that medicine for 17 years from the date of the patent. Drug patents allow prescription-drug companies to set whatever price they choose for a new drug without fear of being undercut by another competitor for nearly two decades. Likewise, trademarks that make it into our everyday vernacular also make it difficult for other companies to compete. For example, no one can make a facial tissue called Kleenex® besides Kimberly Clark and no one can create cotton swabs called Q-Tips® besides Unilever.

Economic moats can sometimes be difficult to quantify or assign an economic value to, but having any of these competitive advantages is preferable to not having them at all. Morningstar has attempted to create a system that ranks a public company's economic moat as wide (strong), narrow (weak), or non-existent. I generally take Morningstar's economic moat ratings with a grain of salt, but they can be a helpful indicator of whether or not a company has any meaningful competitive advantages.

Dividend Analysis Example: Verizon Wireless

In this chapter, we have looked at a number of quantitative and qualitative metrics that we can use to determine whether or not any given dividend stock is attractive. We will now take these newly acquired analytical skills and use them to evaluate a couple of publicly traded companies. Let's start with Verizon (VZ). The company currently pays a dividend yield of 4.27%, which is well within the 3.5–6.5% range that I target. The company has raised its dividend for nine years in a row, which is not quite the 10-year track record that I look for, but is close enough for all intents and purposes. The company has only raised its dividend by an average of 3.2% per year over the last three years, which does not meet the 5–10% annual dividend-growth guideline I target. The company has a healthy payout ratio of about 64%, which is under the 75% maximum payout ratio that I target.

Verizon has a relatively high debt-to-equity ratio of 5.894, which is much higher than the debt-to-equity ratios of competitors AT&T and T-Mobile. The company has averaged net margins of 7.03% over the last five years, which is above the 5% minimum that I require. Verizon has a very high average return on equity of 45.9%, which is largely the result of the amount of debt the company carries. As I write this chapter, the stock is trading at $52.88 and it is trading slightly above its Morningstar fair value estimate of $50.00. Verizon, like most companies you will analyze, won't meet 100% of the criteria that we outline in this chapter, but it comes pretty close. My two big concerns about Verizon are its relatively low dividend-growth rate of 3.2% and the amount of debt the company carries relative to its competitors. These aren't deal breakers given Verizon's already-competitive dividend yield and its ability to manage its debt, but I probably wouldn't call it a "top pick," either.

Dividend Analysis Example: Realty Income Corp

Another favorite stock among dividend investors is Realty Income Corp (O). The company currently pays out an annual dividend of $2.42, which works out to a yield of 3.65% based on a share price of $66.27. The company has raised its dividend every year for the last 20 years and has a dividend payout ratio of 85%, which is to be expected because the company is a real-estate investment trust. It has raised its dividend by an average of 8.6% per year over the last three years, which is an extremely attractive dividend-growth rate. Realty Income Corp has a very healthy debt-to-equity ratio of 0.73:1 and very healthy net margins of 27.97%. The company has an average return on equity of 6.62%, which is acceptable but lower than some of its competitors.

Overall, Realty Income Corp's dividend yield and its track record of paying steadily growing, sustainable dividends make it very attractive to dividend investors. The only major downside for the company is that so many investors have identified it as a solid company that its price has risen dramatically over the last year. It's trading near the top of its 52-week range and it currently has a P/E ratio of more than 60. It is also trading at 130% of its Morningstar fair value estimate. I personally own shares of Realty Income Corp, but probably wouldn't add on to my position until the stock price recedes much closer to its Morningstar fair value estimate.

Dividend Analysis Example: Spectra Energy Partners

Spectra Energy Partners (SEP) is a master limited partnership (MLP) that I personally own shares of. SEP operates liquid natural gas pipelines in the Northeastern and Southeastern United States. The partnership currently pays a very healthy dividend yield of 5.85% and has raised its dividend by an average of 8% over the last three years. SEP has a dividend-payout ratio of 82%, which is not unusual for an energy MLP. The partnership has raised its dividend for nine consecutive years in a row, which is not quite the track record I desire, but SEP's current management appears to be strongly committed to its dividend.

The company's earnings have been growing at a healthy clip, despite the recent dip in energy prices. SEP's debt-to-equity ratio averages about 1.7, which is very reasonable given that SEP operates in an infrastructure-heavy industry. The partnership currently has an attractive net margin of 46.44% and a return on equity of about 11%. Spectra Energy Partners is an example of a company that I currently find very attractive. It's only trading at 91% of its Morningstar fair value estimate and it has an extremely healthy dividend yield of 5.85%. It has been steadily raising its dividend every year and its other financial metrics are generally in line with where they should be.

A Note About These Examples

Please note that the numbers used in these three example analyses were based on a single snapshot in time when I wrote this chapter in September, 2016. The numbers and future prospects for each of these companies have almost certainly changed since I wrote the book.

If you are considering buying or selling any of these stocks, please do your own independent analysis of each of the stocks based on their current financials before making a trade. My personal view of any of these companies may have changed since I wrote this chapter in September, 2016.

By reading through these three examples, I hope you will begin to use the qualitative and quantitative metrics outlined in this chapter as general evaluation guidelines when considering trading dividend stocks. There probably won't be many companies that fall exactly into the cookie-cutter ranges that I suggest for each metric, but there are many great dividend stocks that will fall into the suggested ranges I offer for most metrics. The key is to evaluate a company's dividend yield, number of years of dividend growth, average annual dividend growth, average earnings growth, dividend payout ratio, debt-to-equity ratio, net margins, return on equity, and fair value estimate and determine whether or not each metric is attractive and makes sense for the company given the industry that it is in.

Dividend Evaluation Checklist:

❏ Dividend Yield: Ideally Between 3.5% and 6.5%

❏ Number of Consecutive Years of Dividend Growth: Ideally At Least 10

❏ Average Annual Dividend Growth: Ideally between 5% and 10%

❏ Average Annual Earnings Growth: Ideally in line with or above dividend-growth rates.

❏ Dividend Payout Ratio: Ideally less than 75%, except for REITs and MLPs

❏ Debt to Equity Ratio: Ideally 1:1 or less

❏ Net Margins: Ideally at least 5%

❏ Return on Equity: Ideally at least 10%

❏ Fair Value Estimate: Ideally trading below Morningstar's Fair Value Estimate

CHAPTER FOUR

How to Discover Great Dividend Stocks

YOU NOW KNOW THE qualitative and quantitative metrics that investors should use to measure the quality of a dividend stock, but how do you find attractive dividend stocks that meet the criteria in chapter three? In the past, you may have had to start out with a spreadsheet of the 5,000 stocks that are publicly traded in the United States and test each company against the listed criteria. Fortunately, there are now several websites, tools, and lists that cater to dividend investors, which make it very easy to identify great dividend stocks.

Dividend Lists

Over the last several decades, Standard and Poor's, NAS-DAQ, and a number of other companies have attempted to create models that identify best-of-breed dividend stocks. Each of these stock lists has specific requirements for companies to be listed, such as having raised their dividend every year for a minimum number of years, having a certain minimum market cap and meeting specific capital requirements. These lists, such as the S&P Dividend Aristocrats, provide a good starting point for anyone looking to create a portfolio of dividend stocks, because every company included in these lists has consistently raised their dividend for many years in a row.

S&P Dividend Aristocrats

The S&P Dividend Aristocrats list is a list of S&P 500 companies that have raised their dividend every year for at least the last 25 years. To be included in the list, companies must have a minimum market cap of $3 billion and an average daily trading volume of $5 million. As of 2016, there are currently 52 companies listed on the S&P Dividend Aristocrats list. You can view a list of the companies currently included on the SP Dividend Aristocrats list at www.marketbeat.com/dividends/aristocrats/.

S&P Dow Jones Indices tracks the performance of the S&P 500 Dividend Aristocrats through an equal-weighted index of the companies that are currently on the list. This index has outperformed the S&P 500 by a wide margin over the last decade. Over the 10-year period ending in September, 2016, the S&P 500 Dividend Aristocrats has earned annualized returns of 10.68% per year. This is particularly impressive given that the S&P 500 returned average annualized returns of just 7.5% during the same period. Not only has the S&P 500 Dividend Aristocrats index outperformed the S&P 500 index, it has done so with lower volatility and lower risk. You can track the ongoing performance of the S&P Dividend Aristocrats index at http://us.spindices.com/indices/strategy/sp-500-dividend-aristocrats.

Why has the S&P 500 Dividend Aristocrats Index dramatically outperformed the S&P 500 Index over the last decade? First, companies that pay strong dividends are likely to be generating strong earnings and cash flow that support their above-average dividend payments. Second, a company that pays dividends has to be more selective about how they reinvest earnings into their businesses, because a portion of the company's cash flow is paid out in dividends. Because capital allocation must be more heavily scrutinized in dividend-paying businesses, questionable growth initiatives that are unlikely to create shareholder value do not get funded. Finally, many would argue that the companies listed in the S&P Dividend Aristocrats Index are simply higher-quality companies on average. For a company to have the earnings and cash flow to support increasing its dividend for 25 consecutive years, it must have an economic moat or other competitive advantage that allows it to outperform its competitors.

NASDAQ Dividend Achievers Index

The NASDAQ Dividend Achievers Index is a list of 274 companies that have raised their dividend each year for at least the last 10 years. To be included in the Dividend Achievers Index, a company must be a member of the NASDAQ US Benchmark Index and meet certain minimum capitalization and liquidity requirements. You can view a list of companies that are currently included in the Dividend Achievers Index at www.marketbeat.com/dividends/achievers/.

The companies listed in the Dividend Achievers Index have similar qualities to the companies listed in the S&P 500

Dividend Aristocrats Index. They have a track record of steadily raising their dividends, they have earnings and cash flow to support their dividend payments, and they have lower volatility than the broader market.

The major difference is that the companies in the Dividend Achievers Index do not have as long of a track record of raising their dividends as those in the Dividend Aristocrats Index do. It may be tempting to focus exclusively on the companies that are in the Dividend Aristocrats Index because of their long track records of dividend growth, but I think this is a mistake.

There are many great dividend stocks listed on the Dividend Achievers Index that offer high yields, have strong growth prospects, and are well on their way to being included in the Dividend Aristocrats Index that should be considered for your portfolio as well.

David Fish's Dividend Champions List

Like the S&P Dividend Aristocrats Index, the Dividend Champions List is a list of companies that have raised their dividends for 25 consecutive years. The Dividend Champions list is compiled by David Fish of Moneypaper's DirectInvesting.com. The major difference between the two indexes is that the Dividend Champions list does not include the capital and liquidity requirements of the Dividend Aristocrats Index.

In addition to the 52 companies on the Dividend Aristocrats Index, the Dividend Champions includes an additional 57 companies that do not meet the capital requirements of the Dividend Aristocrats Index. These additional companies either have market caps of less than $3 billion or trade less than an average of $5 million worth of shares each day. The companies currently listed on the Dividend Champions list can be accessed at www.dripinvesting.org/tools/tools.asp.

David Fish also maintains two other dividend lists. His Dividend Challengers list includes companies that have raised their dividend every year for at least the last five years but not more than 10 years. His Dividend Contenders list includes companies that have raised their dividend every year for at least the last 10 years but not more than 24 years.

David Fish regularly publishes updates about the Dividend Challengers List, the Dividend Contenders List, and the Dividend Champions list on SeekingAlpha at www.seekingalpha.com/author/david-fish/articles.

Dividend Kings

The Dividend Kings list includes companies that have raised their dividend every year for more than 50 consecutive years. Companies that have a track record of raising their dividend each year for more than five decades have competitive advantages that stand the test of time.

As of the publishing of this book, there are currently 18 companies listed on the Dividend Kings list, including American States Water (AWR), Cincinnati Financial (CINF), Colgate-Palmolive (CL), Dover Corporation (DOV), Emerson Electric (EMR), Farmers & Merchants Bancorp (FMCB), Genuine Parts Company (GPC), Hormel Foods (HRL), Johnson & Johnson (JNJ), Coca-Cola (KO), Lancaster Colony (LANC), Lowe's (LOW), 3M (MMM), Nordson (NDSN), Northwest Natural Gas (NWN), Parker-Hannifin (PH), Procter & Gamble (PG), and Vectren (VVC).

A Warning About Using Dividend Lists

The lists of dividend stocks mentioned in this chapter are a good starting point for your research, but you should not buy a stock simply because it is included in an index of dividend stocks. Some of the companies in the Dividend Aristocrats index and the Dividend Achievers index actually have lower dividend yields than the S&P 500. None of these lists require a company to have a minimum dividend yield or a minimum amount of dividend growth each year. Some companies will raise their dividend by a token amount each year to maintain their status on these lists while offering low yields. For example, C. R. Bard (BCR) is included on the S&P Dividend Aristocrats Index despite having a dividend yield of just 0.5% and Dover Corp is included on the S&P Dividend Aristocrats Index despite only growing its dividend by an average of 3.3% per year. While dividend lists are a good place to start looking for companies to invest in, make sure that the dividend stocks you buy meet the other recommended criteria outlined in the last chapter.

Dividend Tools on MarketBeat.com

As someone who personally invests in dividend stocks and operates an investment-research website, I am in the unique position of knowing what types of tools dividend investors need and having the ability to actually create them. As a result, we've put together a number of research tools specifically geared toward dividend-stock investors. We make these tools available to everyone for free through our website. You don't even have to give us your email address to use them. Here are the dividend research tools on our website that you might want to make use of:

- **Dividend Screener** – Our dividend screener tool allows you to screen companies by a variety of factors that are important to dividend investors, such as dividend yield, payout ratio, average annual dividend growth, number of consecutive years of dividend growth, and a number of other factors. This tool is probably the best shortcut you have available to finding great dividend stocks that meet the criteria outlined in chapter three. You can access MarketBeat's dividend screener at www.marketbeat.com/dividends/screener/.

- **Dividend Announcements** – MarketBeat keeps track of dividend announcements as they are made in real time. You can use our dividend-announcements calendars each day to view a complete list of publicly traded companies that have announced new dividends. You can easily scan through the list to see if any companies you own have announced new dividends. MarketBeat's dividend-announcements list is available at www.marketbeat.com/dividends/latest.

- **Ex-Dividend Calendar** – Use this calendar to view a list of stocks that are going ex-dividend over the next several days. This is particularly helpful if you're looking at stocks to buy and want to get your first dividend payment soon after you make your purchase. You can access MarketBeat's ex-dividend calendar at www.marketbeat.com/dividends/ex/latest.

- **High-Yield Stocks** – You can view a list of companies that offer particularly high yields using this report. While high yields may seem enticing, make sure to confirm a company's ability to pay its dividend by looking at its payout ratio and earnings growth before making a purchase. You can access MarketBeat's high-yield stocks list at www.marketbeat.com/dividends/high-yield.

- **Dividend Achievers and Dividend Aristocrats** – We provide an up-to-date list of dividend achievers and dividend aristocrats on the MarketBeat website. You can access the Dividend Aristocrats list at www.marketbeat.com/dividends/aristocrats/ and the Dividend Achievers list at www.marketbeat.com/dividends/achievers/.

- **Company Profiles** – One of the features that we are proudest of on the MarketBeat website is our company profiles. For any publicly traded company, you can look up a full history of that company's analyst recommendations, earnings announcements, dividend announcements, insider trades, and headlines. You can also view a stream of recent news about a company and view recent social-media mentions for a company on StockTwits. Our company profile pages include a full description of each company's business model, a number of important financial metrics, and an advanced charting tool. You can look up any publicly traded company's profile page at www.marketbeat.com/stocks.

- **MarketBeat Daily Premium** – This is the only resource included in this list that isn't free. MarketBeat Daily Premium is our premium email newsletter that allows you to create a watch list of stocks that you follow and receive a full summary of every important news item that you would want to know about your companies a full 30 minutes before the market opens. You'll also receive a full run-down of each day's analyst ratings, dividend announcements, earnings announcements, and insider trades. You can also opt to receive instant email or SMS alerts so that we can notify you whenever one of your companies announces a new dividend or is the subject of an important news story. MarketBeat Daily Premium is normally available for $15.97 per month, but readers of this book can subscribe for just $9.97 using this special link: www.bit.ly/marketbeatdailypremium.

Morningstar Dividend Investor

One of my favorite resources to research dividend stocks is the Morningstar Dividend Investor (MDI) newsletter published by Josh Peters, who is a Chartered Financial Analyst and is the director of equity-income strategy at Morningstar, and David Harrel, the managing editor of Morningstar Dividend Investor. MDI is a monthly newsletter that's available for $189.00 per year. While this resource is a bit costlier than some stock research tools, it's well worth the value.

The main feature of the newsletter is the Morningstar Dividend Select Portfolio, which is a model portfolio of approximately 25 dividend-growth stocks managed by Peters. Peters has been managing this portfolio since 2005 and it has yielded total returns of 176.5% through March 2016, compared to the S&P 500 which has offered a total return of 119.5% during the same period. The goal of Morningstar's Dividend Select Portfolio is to earn annual returns of 9%–11% over any three-to-five-year rolling time period. The portfolio also seeks to minimize risk, which they define as the probability of a permanent loss of capital. The Dividend Select Portfolio targets companies that have a 3%–5% current dividend yield and annual dividend-growth rates of 5%–7%; however the portfolio does contain a couple of stocks that have dipped below a 3% yield and holds a few stocks that have yields above 5%. The MDI Dividend Select Portfolio is targeted toward investors that keep their funds in a taxable account, but Morningstar has recently started publishing a second model portfolio that excludes master limited partnerships (MLPs), which is suitable for IRAs, self-directed 401Ks, and other types of retirement accounts.

The monthly MDI newsletter contains a number of other helpful sections for dividend investors. The newsletter contains a cover story which discusses recent news in the world of dividend investing. It also includes a monthly update that discusses the recent performance of the Dividend Select Portfolio as well as brief updates for each stock included in the portfolio. The newsletter also provides a deep-dive research report on two or more of the companies included in the newsletter each month. Finally, MDI includes a section titled "income bellwethers" which discusses other dividend stocks that are not in the Dividend Select Portfolio and a section titled "payouts in peril" which discusses companies whose dividends may get cut in the near future.

More information about Morningstar Dividend Investor can be found at http://mdi.morningstar.com.

SureDividend.com

SureDividend.com is a website that provides educational information about dividend investing and analysis of individual dividend stocks. Publisher Ben Reynolds does a great job of going behind the numbers and really analyzing the business model and future growth prospects for any given stock. He also writes great educational content that teaches readers how think about dividend investing and how to analyze dividend stocks.

Reynolds teaches a set of guidelines that dividend investors should follow, known as the "8 Rules of Dividend Investing." There's a lot of merit to these rules and they are worth repeating in this book. Here are Reynolds' eight rules:

1. **The Quality Rule:** Only invest in high-quality businesses that have a proven track record of long-term stability, growth, and profitability. Only buy stocks that have 25 or more years of dividend payments without a reduction. Reynolds notes that the Dividend Aristocrats have outperformed the S&P 500 by 2.88% per year over the last decade.

2. **The Bargain Rule:** Invest in stocks that pay you the highest dividend yield so that you can create a larger dividend income stream. Focus on companies that have higher-yields compared to other dividend stocks. Reynolds notes that the highest–yielding quintile of stocks has outperformed the lowest-yielding quintile of stocks by 1.76% per year between 1928 and 2013.

3. **The Safety Rule:** Invest in businesses that take in more in cash flow than they send out in dividend payments so that the dividend won't be cut during a downturn. Focus on stocks that have relatively low payout ratios compared to other dividend stocks. Reynolds notes that high-yield, low-payout-ratio stocks have outperformed high-yield, high-payout-ratio stocks by 8.2% between 1990 and 2006.

4. **The Growth Rule:** Invest in companies that have a history of solid earnings growth over a long period of time. Focus on stocks that have solid long-term dividend growth and earnings growth. Reynolds notes that stocks with growing dividends have outperformed stocks with flat dividends by 2.4% per year between 1972 and 2013.

5. **The Peace of Mind Rule:** Invest in companies that do well during recessions and other times of market panic. These types of businesses tend to have relatively stable stock prices and make them easier to hold over the long-term. Focus on stocks that have lower long-term volatility and beta compared to the rest of the market. Reynolds notes that the S&P Low Volatility Index outperformed the S&P500 by 2.00% per year for the 20-year period ending September 30th, 2011.

6. **The Over-Priced Rule:** If you can sell a stock for more than it's worth, you should. When a company has a normalized P/E ratio of more than 40, sell the stock and invest it into a company that has higher-paying dividends. Reynolds notes that the lowest decile of P/E stocks outperformed the highest decile by 9.02% per year between 1975 and 2010.

7. **The Survival of the Fittest Rule:** If a company reduces or eliminates its dividend, you should sell it immediately. Reynolds notes that companies that reduced or eliminated their dividends had a 0% return from 1972 through 2013.

8. **The Hedge Your Bets Rule:** No one is right 100% of the time. Spread your investments over multiple stocks to reduce the impact of being wrong about any one stock. Reynolds notes that you can get 90% of the benefits of diversification that you would get by owning a mutual fund by buying between 12 and 18 stocks.

Reynolds' "8 Rules of Dividend Investing" are worth heeding. While I don't follow them exactly, they provide a great set of starting guidelines for any new dividend investor. Reynolds and I differ in that I am willing to buy stocks with a shorter track record (5–10 years of dividend growth vs. his requirement of 25-year dividend growth) in exchange for higher yields. Most of the stocks he recommends have a 2.5%–4% dividend yield, whereas I tend to focus on companies that have yields above that.

Reynolds also publishes a monthly newsletter, simply referred to as the Sure Dividend Newsletter, that costs $79.00 per year. His monthly newsletter contains a cover story that discusses the overall state of the market as well as a list of 10 top-ranked dividend stocks that he would invest new money into today. Reynolds uses a proprietary formula to calculate which companies make his rankings. The companies he recommends tend to have very low payout ratios, solid long-term track records of dividend growth, and relatively low volatility (beta). The only downside to focusing heavily on these metrics is that he primarily recommends very established stocks that do not offer extremely compelling yields. In his most recent newsletter, the highest-yield stock that is recommended yields just 4.3%. While Reynolds and I focus on stocks with different levels of yield and risk, I do personally subscribe to and read his newsletter each month.

You can learn more about SureDividend at www.suredividend.com.

Dividend.com

Dividend.com is another great resource for researching dividend stocks. While the website does publish news and offers a paid monthly newsletter, the best features of the website are its screening and research tools. Dividend.com has a suite of more than 20 screeners and other research tools that allow you to identify great dividend stocks and build income-generating portfolios. Dividend.com uses a proprietary ranking called DARS, which stands for the Dividend Advantage Rating System, to determine which dividend stocks are the most attractive. Dividend.com includes their DARS rating as a column in each of their screeners.

Some of the screeners and stock recommendations can be accessed for free using the Dividend.com website, but some features are hidden behind a paywall. Their premium section includes a watch list that allows you to keep track of your dividend stocks; a monthly newsletter, access to DARS rankings, and other premium content. Dividend.com offers two subscription options, which are priced at $99 per year and $149 per year, respectively. Dividend.com does also offer a 14-day free trial for new investors.

You can learn more about Dividend.com at www.dividend. com.

Seeking Alpha

Seeking Alpha is the one website that doesn't focus exclusively on dividends that I frequent pretty regularly. If you're reading this book, you probably already visit Seeking Alpha on a semi-regular basis. If for some reason you're not familiar with Seeking Alpha, I'll explain here: it's a publishing platform that allows anyone to become a stock analyst and write about the stocks that they're interested in. While the quality can vary somewhat from article to article, some of the best individual stock analysis I have found is through Seeking Alpha. Because there are dozens of different people writing about any given stock, you can easily read multiple perspectives about a stock in one place.

Whenever I'm researching a new company to invest in, I look up that company on Seeking Alpha and read the 10 most recent articles published about that company. By taking the time to read the most recent analytical pieces on a company, you can usually get a good idea of the company's future growth prospects, the stability of its dividend, and any future clouds that may be on the horizon.

You can visit Seeking Alpha at www.seekingalpha.com.

Wrap-Up

I have mentioned many different resources in this chapter and I personally use all of the tools and lists discussed to identify potential dividend-stock purchases. Remember that these research tools, websites, and resources are a good starting point to identify quality dividend stocks, but they are not a replacement for doing your own analysis. Whenever you trade a dividend stock, you should understand the company's business model, whether or not it has a sustainable and growing dividend, what the company's future growth prospects look like, whether or not the stock is currently overvalued, and whether or not you think that you're buying a fundamentally good company.

CHAPTER FIVE

Taxation of Dividend Stocks

LET'S IMAGINE THAT YOU are considering four different investments that all pay a 4.5% dividend yield: a municipal-bond fund, a blue-chip dividend stock, a master limited partnership (MLP), and a real-estate-investment trust (REIT). The municipal bond fund is not taxable and the after-tax yield will be 4.5%. Dividends from a blue-chip stock are taxed at capital-gains rates and the after tax yield will be 3.825% if your capital gains are taxed at 15%. The MLP will also generate an after-tax yield of 3.825% but no tax will be due until you sell your interest in the MLP. The REIT is taxed at your ordinary tax rate. If you were in the 28% tax bracket, you would earn an after-tax yield of 3.24% on the REIT.

These percentage differences may not seem like much, but the difference between a 3.24% after-tax yield and a 4.5% after-tax yield is the difference between living on $45,000 per year in retirement and $32,400 in retirement if you had a $1 million investment portfolio. The tax treatment of different types of investments that you buy may be confusing at first, but learning how specific types of investments are taxed is extremely important because of the uneven tax burden that is placed on different types of investment income.

A Brief History of Taxes on Dividend Payments in the United States

Prior to 2003, qualified dividends were taxed at the same rates as ordinary income. It didn't matter whether you received investment income from a corporate bond, a savings account, or a dividend stock, you would pay have to pay your ordinary tax rate on your income. The lone exception to this rule was municipal bonds, which are tax free under almost all circumstances.

Then President Bush proposed eliminating the U.S. dividend tax, saying that "double taxation is bad for our economy and falls especially hard on retired people." He also argued that "it's fair to tax a company's profits, [but] it's not fair to double tax by taxing the shareholder on the same profits." Congress passed the Jobs and Growth Tax Relief Reconciliation Act of 2003 soon after. While Congress didn't totally eliminate the dividend tax, they did make the dividend tax rate the same as the capital-gains tax rate, which was 15% for most individual taxpayers at the time. Dividend income for filers in the 10% bracket or the 15% bracket would have their dividends taxed at 5% through 2007.

The lower dividend tax rates were set to expire at the end of 2008, but the Tax Increase Prevention and Reconciliation Act of 2005 extended the lower tax rate through 2010 and cut the tax rate on qualified dividends to 0% for filers in the 10% and 15% income tax brackets. In 2010, President Obama signed the Tax Relief, Unemployment Insurance Reauthorization, and Job Creation Act of 2010 which extended the lower dividend tax rates through 2012.

Many of the Bush-era tax cuts were set to expire at the end of 2012, which would have raised tax rates from 10%, 15%, 25%, 28%, 33% and 35% back to Clinton-era rates of 15%, 28%, 31%, 36%, and 39.6% percent. Had all of the Bush-era tax cuts been allowed to expire, qualified dividends would no longer be taxed at favorable capital-gains rates, but would have been taxed as ordinary income. Fortunately, Congress realized that it wasn't in the best interest of the economy to raise everyone's taxes across the board. Through a compromise in Congress, most households were able to maintain their lower tax rates. The lone exception was individuals that made more than $400,000 per year or families that made more than $450,000 per year, whose top tax rate rose from 35% to 39.6%. Individuals and families in the top tax rate would pay a new capital gains and dividend rate of 20%, up from 15% previously.

Under today's tax code, filers in the 10% and 15% brackets pay no tax on their qualified dividend income. Most individuals pay 15% tax on dividend income and filers in the top tax bracket pay a 20% tax rate on qualified dividend income rates. In addition to the normal dividend tax, the Affordable Care Act of 2012 instituted a new 3.8% net investment income tax that applies to dividends, capital gains, and other kinds of passive investment income which is charged to single filers that make more than $200,000 per year and joint filers that make more than $250,000 per year. This means you could pay a dividend tax rate as low as zero if you don't have much of an income or a dividend tax rate as high as 23.8% if you are in the top tax bracket.

Please note that Congress tends to change tax laws pretty regularly. New tax legislation may have changed dividend tax rates since this book was published. If you are reading this book more than a year after it was published, you should confirm independently that dividend tax rates have not changed.

What are Qualified Dividends?

In order for a dividend payment to be considered a qualified dividend and be taxed at preferential capital-gains rates, it must meet a few basic criteria. The dividend payment must have been paid by an American or a foreign qualifying company. A foreign corporation is considered qualified if it is incorporated in the United States, it is eligible for the benefits of a comprehensive income tax treaty with the United States, or if the stock is readily tradable on an established securities market in the United States.

The recipient of the dividend payment must also have held the underlying stock for a specific period of time in order for a dividend to be considered qualified. The required holding period for common stock is 60 days during the 121-day period that starts 60 days before the ex-dividend date. The required holding period for preferred stock is more than 90 days during a 181-day period that starts 90 days before the ex-dividend date. These rules are effectively designed to disincentivize short-term trading by using lower tax rates to reward dividend investors that hold shares for a longer period of time.

Finally, there are some types of dividend payments that are explicitly excluded from receiving qualified dividend rates. Dividends paid by real estate investment trusts (REITs), master limited partnerships (MLPs), employee stock options, tax-exempt companies, and money-market accounts do not receive qualified dividend treatment and are taxed as ordinary income.

Special one-time dividends also do not receive qualified dividend treatment. You should not avoid REITs, MLPs, and other investments that do not receive qualified tax treatment, but you should consider what tax rate you will be paying when making an investment.

These rules may sound complicated, but most dividends that you receive by investing in companies like Coca-Cola, General Electric, AT&T, Apple, and Wal-Mart will be qualified dividends as long as you're not regularly trading in and out of positions.

Taxation of Dividends on International Stocks

As an investor that is targeting both income and diversification, you may look to international dividend stocks to add to your portfolio. There are many companies outside of the United States that offer consistent dividend payments and dividend growth. However, you can't always compare a 5% yield in another country to a 5% yield in the United States. Many foreign countries see dividend payments to international investors as an easy source of tax revenue and charge foreign investors dividend tax rates between 5% and 30% on dividend payments. Foreign governments collect tax payments on dividends before they are delivered to your brokerage account, because they know compliance rates would be almost zero if investors had to mail in tax payments. Some countries, such as the United Kingdom, India, and Argentina do not tax dividends paid to U.S. investors due to various tax treaties that the United States has with those countries.

Here is a current breakdown of international dividend tax rates by country:

Country	Rate	Country	Rate
Australia	30%	Macedonia	10%
Austria	25%	Malaysia	25%
Bangladesh	15%	Malta	35%
Belgium	25%	Mexico	10%
Bosnia	5%	Morocco	10%
Brazil	15%	The Netherlands	15%
Bulgaria	15%	New Zealand	30%
Canada	15%	Nigeria	10%
Chile	35%	Norway	25%
China	10%	Pakistan	10%
Czech Republic	15%	Peru	4.10%
Denmark	28%	Philippines	30%
Finland	28%	Poland	19%
France	25%	Portugal	20%
Germany	26.40%	Romania	16%
Greece	10%	Russia	15%
Hungary	10%	Saudi Arabia	5%
Iceland	15%	Serbia	20%
Indonesia	20%	Slovenia	20%
Ireland	20%	South Korea	27.50%
Israel	20%	Spain	19%
Italy	27%	Sri Lanka	10%
Japan	10%	Sweden	30%
Kazakhstan	15%	Switzerland	35%
Kenya	10%	Taiwan	20%
Kuwait	15%	Thailand	10%
Latvia	10%	Turkey	15%
Lebanon	10%	United Kingdom (REITs only)	20%
Lithuania	15%		
Luxembourg	15%	Ukraine	15%

Fortunately, there may be a way to recoup some or all of the taxes collected on your dividend payments by foreign credits. The U.S. tax code includes a credit for tax payments made to foreign governments, simply known as the foreign tax credit. The purpose of this credit is to avoid double taxation of income by two separate companies. In other words, the IRS doesn't want to tax you on dividend income that you've already been taxed on by a foreign government. Note that there are limitations to the amount of foreign-tax payments you can take as a credit, so you may not be able to receive a credit for 100% of the tax that you paid to a foreign government. Regulations regarding the foreign tax credit are complex, so check with a qualified financial professional if you plan to take the foreign tax credit. You can learn more about the foreign tax credit at https://www.irs.gov/individuals/international-taxpayers/foreign-tax-credit-how-to-figure-the-credit.

Other than tax considerations, you should also consider currency risks, political risks, and regulatory risks before investing in foreign dividend stocks. Acts of terrorism, war, civil unrest, natural disasters, and other calamities can significantly change the economic outlook of a country and the companies that operate within its borders. A foreign government could also impose new taxes on dividend payments, or the companies you invest in may be nationalized by a country's government. Significant changes in currency values could also affect the value of your foreign stocks if they are not priced in U.S. dollars. Because of these risks, I tend to only invest in companies that are located in countries that have well established and stable governments, like the United Kingdom and Canada.

Another important consideration regarding investing in international dividend stocks is that they often do not mirror the monthly or quarterly payment schedules that are common in

U.S. dividend stocks. For example, National Grid Plc (NGG) only pays out dividends twice per year and its May dividend is often twice as much as its November dividend. Some foreign stocks will also vary the amount of their dividend based on the company's actual profits, so make sure to research the company's dividend payment history using MarketBeat's company profiles or another resource to verify a foreign company's frequency of dividend payments and consistency of dividend amounts.

If you are considering buying a foreign dividend stock and want to place a trade, you may find out that you aren't able to place trades on many exchanges outside the United States in your brokerage account. Fortunately, many large foreign companies trade as American Depository Receipts (ADRs) on the New York Stock Exchange, the NASDAQ, and other U.S. exchanges. ADRs are tradable certificates of ownership representing a certain number of shares of a foreign stock issued by a U.S. bank. ADRs are bought and sold like regular shares and are denominated in U.S. currency. They also pay out dividends just like owning the actual shares of a stock would. ADRs effectively provide a very easy way for individual investors in the United States to buy shares of large foreign companies throughout the world.

Taxation of Real-Estate Investment Trusts

As we learned earlier, real-estate investment trusts (REITs) are a special type of corporate entity used for commercial real-estate projects that can avoid paying corporate taxes at the federal level. Because REITs are not set up as a typical C-corporation like most publicly traded companies are, they have special requirements under the tax code. REITs have the same accounting and valuations that corporations do, but instead of distributing profits to shareholders, they distribute cash flow. In fact, the IRS requires REITs to pay out 90% of their income to shareholders as distributions, which means they will generally have higher dividend yields than the common market and they will have very high payout ratios.

When a REIT meets the 90% payout requirement, it is generally exempted from paying corporate taxes at the federal level. Because of this tax provision, distributions from REITs are not considered qualified dividends and are taxed at a shareholder's ordinary income rates. A portion of a REITs distribution may also be considered a non-taxable return of capital, which reduces a shareholder's taxable income in the year it is received and defers payment of taxes on that portion of the investor's shares until they are sold. These payments will also reduce the shareholder's cost basis in the stock. REITs also may pay out some qualified dividends in a few special cases, but generally speaking, most distributions from REITs will be taxed at a shareholder's ordinary tax rate.

The tax treatment of REIT distributions can make them less attractive to investors in high tax brackets. If you are in the top tax bracket, you will pay your ordinary tax rate of 39.6% plus the net investment income tax of 3.8% on any distributions you receive from a REIT. This turns a 5% dividend yield before tax into 2.83% dividend yield after tax. Ouch. When possible, hold your REIT investments in a non-taxable or tax-advantaged investment account, such as an IRA or a 401K, to avoid paying ordinary income taxes on REITs. If this isn't an option for you, just make sure you are considering what after-tax dividend yield you will receive when comparing REITs to other dividend stocks.

Taxation of Master Limited Partnerships (MLPs)

Master limited partnerships (MLPs) are a special type of corporate entity that is a combination of a partnership and a publicly traded company. They are primarily used as corporate vehicles for energy and utilities companies. Since MLPs are pass-through entities, their income is only taxed at the level of the partners in the MLP and is generally not subject to corporate taxes at the federal level. Distributions from MLPs are not subject to tax when they are received by a shareholder. Instead, MLP distributions simply reduce the investor's cost basis in the MLP, which effectively defers all tax payments on distributions until the investor sells their shares in the MLP.

While MLPs offer significant tax benefits to investors, there are two caveats to be aware of. First, you should not invest in an MLP through an IRA or other tax-deferred account. Income from an MLP is not tax-deferred if shares are held in an IRA, which eliminates the tax benefits of investing in MLPs. Second, investing in MLPs may make filing your taxes each year slightly more complicated.

Instead of receiving a 1099 form at the end of the year, you will receive a K-1 form as you would with any other business partnership. This is really only an issue if you do your own taxes, as any qualified tax professional will know how to include the numbers from a K-1 form on your return.

Taxation of Preferred Stocks

Preferred stocks are a special class of shares in a company that pay a fixed dividend yield like a bond does. The tax treatment of dividends paid by preferred stocks can vary from security to security.

Some preferred stocks will pay out qualified dividends just as any other publicly traded company. Dividend payments issued by trust-preferred securities are not qualified dividends because they are essentially interest payments. Preferred-stock dividends issued by business development companies (BDCs) are also not qualified distributions.

Make sure to read the investment prospectus for the pre-ferred-stock issue if you are considering investing in a preferred stock. The preferred-stock issue's prospectus will explain the tax treatment of the stock along with other important investment information.

Taxation of Royalty Income Trusts

Royalty income trusts are a special type of entity that oil and natural gas producers use to provide a secure financing source for the operations of their business. Royalty trusts generate income from the production of natural resources, such as coal, oil, and natural gas. Royalty trusts have no employees, no management, and no operations of their own. They exist strictly to own natural-resource assets and receive royalties from the companies that are harvesting the natural resources they own. Royalty trusts tend to have very high yields because they are required to pay out virtually all of their cash flow as distributions.

Like MLPs, royalty trusts are considered pass-through vehicles and are not subject to corporate tax at the federal level. Distributions from royalty trusts are also not considered taxable income by the IRS because of depreciation and depletion of the underlying natural resources that are owned by the trust. Like MLPs, distributions from royalty trusts reduce an owner's cost basis in the stock and doe not get taxed until the shareholder sells their interest in the stock.

When an investor in a royalty trust sells their interest, they will be taxed at their capital-gains rate based on their final cost basis and the current price of the royalty trust. Investors in royalty trusts may be able to claim unusual tax credits, such as receiving a credit for producing fuel from unconventional sources. These credits generally don't amount to much, but they are a nice fringe to have.

Taxation of Business Development Companies

Business development companies (BDCs) are a special type of corporate entity that was created by Congress in 1980 to encourage public investment in privately held companies. Like REITs, MLPs, and royalty trusts, business development companies are pass-through entities and are not taxed at the corporate level if they pay out 90% of their taxable income each year and derive more than 90% of their income from capital gains, dividends, and interest on securities. Just like with REITs, distributions paid by BDCs are taxed at an investor's ordinary income rates and are not considered qualified dividends. For this reason, BDCs are best held in tax-advantaged accounts like IRAs and self-directed 401Ks.

Using your IRA to Invest in Dividend Stocks

At the beginning of each year, your first investment priority should be maxing out your individual retirement accounts (IRAs), your 401K/403B plan, and any other tax-advantaged investment accounts you may have. Taxes on capital gains and dividends can eat up a significant portion of your investment income when you use a standard brokerage account, so always max out your tax-advantaged investment options before investing through a traditional taxable brokerage account.

You can currently invest $5,500 per year (or $11,000 if you're married) into an IRA. If you're over the age of 50, you can contribute up to $6,500 per year (or $13,000 if you're married). If you want to invest in dividend stocks in an IRA, make sure to sign up for an IRA with a company that allows you to buy and sell individual stocks and not just own mutual funds.

This means you should stick with IRAs set up by discount stock brokerages if you want to trade individual stocks, like TD Ameritrade, and avoid IRAs set up by mutual-fund companies that only permit you to invest in their mutual funds.

There are two distinct types of IRAs. Traditional IRAs allow investors to receive an immediate tax deduction for contributions made to an IRA. However, you will have to pay your ordinary income tax rate on any money you withdraw from your IRA during retirement. Roth IRAs do not offer an up-front tax deduction like a traditional IRA. Any dividends or capital gains earned by investments in your Roth IRA are not taxed and you can withdraw from your Roth IRA at age 59 ½ tax-free. It may be somewhat difficult to determine which choice is optimal for your situation, because you don't know what tax rates will be when you retire and you may not know what tax bracket you will be in during your retirement years. I personally invest in a Roth IRA simply because I would rather pay taxes on money before it benefits from decades of dividend and capital gains, but you may want to consult a financial professional to determine which type of IRA is most appropriate for your situation.

IRAs are perfectly appropriate investment vehicles for most types of securities, including individual stocks, bonds, certificates of deposit, mutual funds, exchange-traded funds, and even real estate. IRAs are also appropriate to hold regular dividend stocks, real-estate investment trusts, royalty trusts, and business-development companies. MLPs are an exception and should not be held in an IRA because they lose their tax benefits when held inside an IRA. You should also not hold collectibles in an IRA, including artwork, antiques, gems, stamps, and coins. Finally, you cannot hold life insurance policies in an IRA and you cannot buy securities on margin inside of an IRA.

If you are above the income limit to contribute to an IRA each year, you may still be able to contribute to a Roth IRA because of a tax loophole that allows you to contribute to a non-deductible IRA and immediately convert it into a Roth IRA. This loophole is commonly referred to as a "backdoor Roth IRA." There are specific rules about your non-deductible IRA contributions and when they can be converted into a traditional Roth IRA, so talk to your financial advisor or accountant about how to properly use this strategy before trying to implement it yourself.

Using Employer-Sponsored Retirement Accounts to Invest in Dividend Stocks

After you have maxed out your IRAs, you will then want to move on to any retirement plans you have through your employer such as 401Ks and 403Bs. If you are self-employed, you can set up your own retirement plan through a Simplified Employee Pension (SEP) or through an Individual 401(K). Unfortunately, most employer-sponsored retirement accounts do not permit you to invest in single stocks and give you a limited selection of mutual funds to choose from. If this is the case, I suggest choosing a more traditional age-appropriate asset allocation of stocks and bonds for your 401K plan.

However, some 401K plans do permit you to place the majority of your 401K contribution into a self-directed brokerage account. For example, I recently set up a 401K plan for MarketBeat with Vanguard through a company called Ascensus, which allows me to place 90% of my monthly contribution into a self-directed brokerage account through TD Ameritrade. I primarily use my 401K brokerage account to hold REITs and other income assets that do not pay out qualified dividends.

Using a Health Savings Account for Dividend Investing

One additional tax-advantaged investment account that you may not have considered is a health savings account (HSA). While most people use HSAs to pay for medical expenses with pre-tax money, HSAs can also be used as a tax-advantaged vehicle to set aside money for the future. If you have a qualifying high-deductible health plan, you can currently set aside $6,500 per year inside of an HSA. With your HSA, you will receive an immediate tax deduction for any contributions you make into an HSA. You can then use your HSA balance to pay for medical expenses tax-free or you can invest your HSA in mutual funds and have a "medical IRA" of sorts to pay for future medical expenses you may incur in your life.

You will probably have somewhat limited investment options inside an HSA, but there are HSA accounts that include dividend-growth mutual funds that you can invest in. If you end up not needing the money for medical expenses, you can withdraw the money from your account and pay your ordinary tax rate as you would on a traditional IRA or 401K plan once you hit age 65.

Dividend Investing Through a Traditional Brokerage Account

After you have exhausted all of your tax-advantaged investment accounts, then your next step is to start investing in dividend stocks through a standard taxable brokerage account. There are many perfectly good online discount brokerages that you can use to hold your dividend stock portfolio. When comparing brokerages, consider the fees that you are paying, the types of investments that are available to trade, the research tools that you have access to, the ease-of-use of the broker's website and the brokerage company's track record of customer service. There are many websites which compare brokers to one another, but be aware that many of those websites receive affiliate commissions for recommending certain brokerages over others. Your best bet is to read the marketing material published by each brokerage and use the brokerage that best suits your need.

I personally use a Vanguard brokerage account for my dividend-stock portfolio. While their research tools aren't as good as some other brokerages, they offer fantastic customer service and charge very low fees. I personally receive a few dozen free trades each year and only pay $2.00 per trade after that because I qualify for Vanguard's Voyager Select service. I also have other accounts with Vanguard and prefer to keep our various accounts at one provider. TD Ameritrade is also a very good all-around brokerage. I use them for the self-directed portion of my 401K plan and a small investment club that I am a part of.

Asset Location Matters

If you have different types of investments interspersed between an IRA, a 401k plan, and a taxable brokerage account, make sure to put your investments that receive the poorest tax treatment inside your tax-advantaged accounts in order to minimize your tax burden. This means you always should put tax-free investments, like municipal bonds, inside of your taxable brokerage account. You should put assets that are taxed as ordinary income, such as REITs, BDCs, corporate bonds and some preferred stocks inside your IRA, 401k, or other tax-advantaged accounts whenever possible. Dividend stocks can either be placed in your tax-advantaged or taxable brokerage account, depending on what other assets you may want to place in your tax-advantaged investment accounts.

Wrap-up

As we learned from the example at the beginning of this chapter, taxes can dramatically alter how much of your investment income you actually get to keep. If you were in the top tax bracket, the difference between a tax-free municipal bond and a real-estate investment trust would be 43.4% (39.6% in ordinary income taxes and 3.8% net investment income tax). When reviewing different investments, always compare the after-tax dividend yield that you will receive from each investment and determine which of your investment accounts is the best location to hold each investment.

CHAPTER SIX

How to Build a Dividend Stock Portfolio

YOU NOW HAVE AN understanding of how dividend stocks work, why they are attractive investments, how to evaluate individual dividend stocks, what tools you can use to research dividend stocks, and the tax implications of owning different types of dividend stocks. The only two things left that we need to learn are how to actually create a portfolio of dividend stocks and live during retirement off of the income your portfolio generates up to and during retirement.

What Should a Dividend Portfolio Look Like?

Over time, you should work to build a diversified portfolio of 15–25 dividend stocks in different industries. You will probably own several blue-chip stocks, a couple of real-estate investment trusts (REITs), a master limited partnership (MLP), and some preferred stock or a preferred-stock fund inside of your portfolio. My portfolio consists of 23 S&P 500 companies, two master limited partnerships, three real-estate investment trusts, one preferred stock ETF, and two closed-end municipal-bond funds.

Your portfolio should target a blended dividend yield of 4% to 5% in order to generate attractive dividend payments without taking on too much risk. If you own a typical mix of dividend stocks, your portfolio's beta should be around 0.8, meaning that it is only 80% as volatile as the broader market indexes. You should target a 10% total annual return between capital gains and the dividend payments you receive. Your portfolio's dividend payments should grow by an average of 5% to 8% each year so that the amount of income your portfolio generates increases every year.

I hesitate to discuss specific companies that are frequently included in dividend portfolios, primarily because the future growth prospects of any given company can change over time. For example, Pitney Bowes (PBI) was part of the S&P Dividend Aristocrats list, meaning they had raised their dividend for more than 25 years in a row. In 2013, the company was forced to cut their dividend by more than 50% after years of facing steadily shrinking demand for its shipping and mailing products. If you had read that Pitney Bowes had a long track record of dividend growth and was included in many dividend portfolios in a book written five years earlier, you might not know about that company's fall from grace and add it to your portfolio without doing enough research. If you would like ideas for companies that you may want to include in your portfolio of dividend stocks, consider subscribing to the Morningstar Dividend Investor newsletter, subscribing to the SureDividend newsletter, or using any of the other research tools outlined earlier in this book.

Should You Include Other Investments in Your Income Portfolio?

Ultimately, what we're trying to accomplish by buying dividend-growth stocks is to create an income stream that we can live off of during retirement. Dividend stocks are by far my favorite income-generating investment because they offer both near-term income and long-term capital gains, but they're not the only income-generating investments you might want to consider. Like any other asset class, dividend stocks can come in and out of favor depending on how other income investments are performing and what mood the market happens to be in. In order to create diversification among the asset classes you own, you may also consider buying municipal bonds if you are in a high tax bracket, buying a rental house or a duplex depending on what your local real estate market looks like, or loaning money to other people through peer-to-peer lending websites like Lending Club and Prosper.

In addition to my portfolio of dividend stocks, I personally own shares of two closed-end municipal bond funds that have very attractive tax-equivalent yields. I have invested in a couple of local private-equity deals that throw off income each year. I also had previously invested in consumer notes through Lending Club, which are taxed as ordinary income. I divested my portfolio of Lending Club notes when I found myself in the 39.6% tax bracket and the after-tax yield I was receiving was no longer competitive. Finally, I own a piece of rental real estate that generates positive cash flow each month.

Should I Just Buy a Dividend Mutual Fund?

It can be a lot of work to research individual companies and build a portfolio of 15–25 dividend stocks and you may be tempted to just buy a dividend-growth mutual fund instead. There have been some decent attempts to create dividend funds and ETFs, but they have several downsides that any dividend investor should be aware of.

First, dividend mutual funds tend to have unimpressive yields. Mutual funds have to own a large number of companies in order to remain fully invested in the market. For example, Vanguard's Dividend Growth Fund (VDIGX) has more than $30 billion in assets and is the largest dividend-growth mutual fund in the world. If that fund were to target a few target select dividend-growth stocks, it would literally have to buy entire companies to invest its' shareholder' 'money. Because ETFs and mutual funds have to own so many companies, they end up having to invest in many companies that pay low yields and have unimpressive dividend growth. VDIGX currently pays a yield of just 1.91%, which is actually a lower yield than offered by an S&P 500 index fund.

Dividend mutual funds and ETFs tend to have relatively high expense ratios relative to the low-cost index funds that are now available through Vanguard, Fidelity, and other providers. Expense ratios eat away at the dividend income you receive. For example, the SPDR S&P Dividend ETF (SDY) and the ProShares S&P 500 Dividend Aristocrats ETF each have an expense ratio of 0.35% per year. While that number may seem insignificant, NOBL currently pays a dividend yield of just 2.06%. If you were to own the 52 companies that make up the S&P Dividend Aristocrats Index in your brokerage account at the same weighting at NOBL, you would earn a 2.41% dividend yield because you are not paying the 0.35% expense ratio to the fund's managers. By paying the 0.35% expense ratio, you would be giving up 14.5% of the dividends you would otherwise receive to ProShares in management fees.

When you invest in a dividend mutual fund or ETF, you have no control over what companies are included in your portfolio and which are not. You are stuck with the basket of stocks selected by the fund's managers or by the index that the fund tracks. You are unable to model the portfolios outlined by Morningstar Dividend Investor, SureDividend, or any other dividend advisory service because those portfolios are not modeled by any existing ETF or mutual fund. While you might select a dividend ETF or mutual fund that has a lot of solid companies that meet the criteria outlined in chapter three, there may be just as many low-yield or low-growth companies in the fund that drag down your portfolio's overall yield and capacity for dividend growth.

The main reason you might consider owning a dividend mutual fund or ETF is diversification, but it turns out that you can get most of the benefits of diversification by owning one or two dozen individual stocks. According to Keith Brown and Frank Reilley, authors of *Investment Analysis and Portfolio Management*, a series of studies for randomly selected stocks show that you can get "about 90% of the maximum benefit of diversification was derived from portfolios of 12 to 18 stocks." These studies do assume that you own an equally weighted portfolio, meaning that you own an equal dollar amount of each stock in your portfolio.

For your personal IRA and your taxable brokerage account, I would choose investing in individual dividend stocks over choosing a dividend mutual fund or ETF, any day of the week. There are two scenarios where it may be a good idea to invest in a dividend ETF or mutual fund. First, if you're investing through a 401K or other retirement plan that only allows you to buy mutual funds, you may choose to invest in a dividend mutual fund to get many of the benefits of dividend growth while operating within the constraints of your retirement account.

The only other scenario where you might consider choosing a dividend mutual fund is if you aren't interested or willing to do the research to select individual dividend stocks yourself and want a much more hands-off approach. In this case, you might be willing to pay a management fee and accept a lower dividend yield than you could get otherwise in order to get the benefits of dividend-growth investing without having to learn about investing and researching individual stocks yourself. Since you're reading a book about dividend investing, I suspect that's not the case in your situation.

Should I Reinvest My Dividends?

Many brokers offer dividend reinvestment programs (DRIPs) which allow you to automatically purchase additional shares of a stock with dividend payments that you receive without having to pay a trade fee. Most major discount brokers offer DRIPs including TradeKing, TD Ameritrade, Scotttrade, E*TRADE, Firsttrade, and Vanguard. If your brokerage offers a DRIP, you will be given the option whether or not to automatically reinvest the dividend payments that you receive. I generally recommend reinvesting your dividends because your money is immediately put back to work to generate additional dividend income and capital gains for you over the long term.

Before you retire and begin to live off your dividend payments, the only other time you might not want to reinvest your dividends is when a stock is particularly overvalued and is no longer attractive for additional purchases. In this case, take your dividend payment as cash and reinvest the funds into dividend stock that is more attractive at the time. You are still reinvesting your dividends, but you are reinvesting the funds in a different company. If a dividend payment doesn't amount to much and you would have to pay a large percentage of the dividend payment as a trade fee, hold on to the money until you have additional funds to invest and would be paying less than 1% of your transaction as a trade fee.

When Should I Sell a Dividend Stock?

Dividend-growth investing is a long-term play and is very much a "buy and hold" strategy. As long as your stocks remain attractive and continue to grow their dividend, you should hold on to them. If a company's dividend gets cut or if there is a very strong possibility of it being cut, you should cut bait and move the money into a more attractive stock. You can determine when a dividend payment becomes unsustainable by regularly tracking your companies' dividend payout ratio (DPR). If any of your stocks DPR rises above 90% (with the exception of REITs and utilities), you should closely monitor them and do additional research to determine if the company's dividend is likely to get cut.

You might also consider selling a stock if you can trade it for a similar company with a better yield, better growth prospects, or a more sustainable dividend. For example, the Morningstar Dividend Investor Dividend Select Portfolio sold shares of AT&T last summer and used the funds to buy shares of Verizon. Both companies offered similar yields, but AT&T's dividend growth had significantly slowed down and Verizon offered much better long-term earnings-growth potential.

Planning Your Retirement Income Stream

When you are nearing retirement and want to begin living off Social Security, your investment portfolio, and other secondary income sources, your first step is to take stock of each potential source of monthly income from your family. If you live in the United States, you will probably receive some income in the form of Social Security. You should calculate how much income your portfolio of dividend stocks will generate each year by multiplying your portfolio value by its blended dividend yield. Also calculate any additional income that you have from other investments, such as rental real-estate or a 401K plan. Total the income you will receive from these various sources and compare that number to what your average monthly living expenses are to see if you are ready to retire.

If these sources together don't cover your living expenses, you may consider taking a low-stress part-time job to fill the gap. This doesn't mean you have to be a greeter at Wal-Mart and you may actually enjoy pursuing a new career path on a part-time basis during your retirement years. There are also great health benefits to staying active and continuing to work part-time during your retirement years that you should take into consideration.

Once you have taken stock of the various income sources available to you in retirement, you then need to identify which sources you will want to withdraw from first. This decision will primarily be driven by taxes and the optimal age to start receiving Social Security. It can be advantageous to hold off on taking Social Security if you are generally healthy and relying on other income sources to delay Social Security. Because of the amount of money involved, it may be worth your time to talk to a Social Security consultant to determine the ideal age for you to begin taking Social Security.

Generally speaking, you should avoid taking money out of retirement accounts until you need the money or are required to take minimum distributions from a retirement account. For any traditional IRA or 401K accounts you have, you will be required to begin taking minimum distributions beginning at age 70 ½. Required minimum distribution rules do not apply to Roth 401Ks or Roth IRAs. You can learn more about required minimum distributions on the IRS website at https://www.irs.gov/retirement-plans/retirement-plans-faqs-regarding-required-minimum-distributions.

Living Off Dividend Payments

When it becomes time to start relying on your dividend investments to pay for your living expenses during your retirement years, you simply need to stop reinvesting your dividend payments and let them collect in your brokerage account. At the end of each month or each quarter, initiate a bank transfer to withdraw the dividend payments you have received and transfer them to your primary bank account and use the funds as you would with any other kind of income.

Remember that you will owe tax on any dividend payments that you receive from companies held in a taxable brokerage account. If you are not in the top tax bracket, you should set aside 15% of the dividend payments you receive for taxes at the end of the year. If you are in the top tax bracket, you should set aside 23.8% of the dividend payments you receive for taxes at the end of the year. In order to minimize any burden from capital gains tax, try to avoid selling any appreciated stocks in your portfolio if at all possible.

Wrap-Up

A lot of ground has been covered in *Automatic Income*. You have learned the basics of how dividend payments work. You now know why dividend stocks are incredibly attractive investments. You have learned about blue chips, REITs, MLPs, royalty trusts, and other types of dividend stocks. You have studied how to research and evaluate dividend stocks. You now know about different resources that we can use to identify high-quality companies to invest in. You have learned about the tax implications of different types of dividend investments. You now know how to build a portfolio of dividend-paying stock and live off that portfolio during retirement.

The next step is for you to start taking action. Open a brokerage account with a discount brokerage firm if you don't already have one. Make a small deposit and purchase your first shares of a dividend-paying stock to see how the process works. Watch as your first few dividend payments come in. Continue learning by reading the resources mentioned in Appendix One and soak in every bit of information you can about dividend investing. Begin doing some of your own research on individual dividend-paying stocks. Develop a savings plan so that you can grow your portfolio of dividend stocks each month and put that plan into action.

As you begin to create and grow your portfolio of dividend stocks, the payments you receive may seem small and inconsequential at first, but remember that they will compound over time. If you were to buy 100 shares of a company today that pays a 4% dividend and that dividend grows by 8% each year at the cost of $10,000, you would have an income stream of $1,184.05 after 10 years if you reinvest your dividends and pay a 15% capital-gains rate. After 20 years, that number would grow to $3,504.91. After 30 years, you would be earning $10,374.94 in dividends per year on your original investment of $10,000. That's the power of dividend investing in action. Now, it's your turn.

APPENDIX ONE

Helpful Resources

THE PURPOSE OF *AUTOMATIC Income* is to provide a solid primer for anyone who wants to learn about dividend investing. I do not expect this book to be the definitive or only resource that you use to learn about investing in dividend stocks. As part of my research for this book, I read many other books on dividend investing, purchased many dividend newsletters, and tried out various dividend-research tools. Below, you'll find a list of the books, newsletters, and resources that I've found helpful in researching dividend stocks. I can't say that I agree with 100% of the recommendations made by any of these resources, but they are helpful tools that will further your educational journey.

Books:

- *The Ultimate Dividend Playbook* by Josh Peters
- *Get Rich with Dividends* by Marc Lichtenfeld
- *Income Investing Secrets* by Richard Stooker
- *The Single Best Investment* by Lowell Miller
- *Dividends Still Don't Lie* by Kelley Wright

Websites:

- Dividend.com (http://www.dividend.com/)
- Dividend Channel (http://www.dividendchannel.com/)
- Dividend Monk (http://www.dividendmonk.com/)
- Drip Investing Resource Center (http://www.dripinvesting.org/)
- Investopedia (http://www.investopedia.com/)
- MarketBeat (http://www.marketbeat.com/)
- Sure Dividend (http://www.suredividend.com/)
- Seeking Alpha (http://www.seekingalpha.com/)

Newsletters:

- Morningstar Dividend Investor (http://mdi.morningstar.com/)
- Sure Dividend's Monthly Newsletter (http://www.suredividend.com/)

APPENDIX TWO

S&P Dividend Aristocrats

THIS IS A LIST of the 52 companies that are included in the S&P Dividend Aristocrats Index as of September, 2016. This list offers a reasonable starting point for anyone looking to research individual dividend stocks and create a portfolio of dividend stocks. Remember that not every company listed in the S&P Dividend Aristocrats Index is an attractive dividend stock. Some companies listed below have low dividend yields and low growth prospects.

3M Company (MMM)	W. W. Grainger (GWW)
AFLAC Inc. (AFL)	HCP (HCP)
AbbVie Inc. (ABBV)	Hormel Foods Corp (HRL)
Abbott Laboratories (ABT)	Illinois Tool Works (ITW)
Air Products & Chemicals Inc (APD)	Johnson & Johnson (JNJ)
Archer-Daniels-Midland Co (ADM)	Kimberly-Clark (KMB)
AT&T (T)	Leggett & Platt (LEG)
Automatic Data Processing (ADP)	Lowe's Companies, Inc. (LOW)
C. R. Bard (BCR)	McCormick & Company (MKC)
Becton Dickinson (BDX)	McDonald's (MCD)
Bemis Company (BMS)	Medtronic (MDT)
Brown-Forman (Class B shares BF/B)	Nucor (NUE)
Cardinal Health Inc. (CAH)	PPG Industries (PPG)
Chevron Corp. (CVX)	PepsiCo (PEP)
Cincinnati Financial Corp (CINF)	Pentair (PNR)
Cintas Corp (CTAS)	Procter & Gamble (PG)
The Clorox Company (CLX)	S&P Global (formerly McGraw Hill Financial, Inc. SPGI)
Coca-Cola Co (KO)	Sherwin-Williams (SHW)
Colgate-Palmolive (CL)	Sigma-Aldrich (SIAL)
Consolidated Edison Inc (ED)	Stanley Black & Decker Inc. (SWK)
Dover Corp (DOV)	Sysco (SYY)
Ecolab Inc (ECL)	T. Rowe Price (TROW)
Emerson Electric (EMR)	Target Corporation (TGT)
Exxon Mobil Corp (XOM)	VF Corporation (VFC)
Franklin Resources (BEN)	Wal-Mart (WMT)
Genuine Parts Company (GPC)	Walgreen Boots Alliance (WBA)

APPENDIX THREE
Legal Disclaimers

I AM NOT A stock broker or a licensed securities dealer or a representative of any kind. I have no legal right to sell securities of any kind nor am I attempting to do so. Nothing in this book should be considered a solicitation or offer to sell you securities of any kind.

Nothing in this book should be considered professional financial advice. I do not know you or your situation and am not making any specific recommendations to your situation. I am not a registered investment advisor or a financial advisor of any kind. I do not offer personal financial advice in this book. Please consult a qualified financial professional before buying or selling any securities.

This book is based on my personal research and believed to be accurate. It consists of my ideas, opinions, and suggestions. I have attempted to verify all of the information in this book, but cannot guarantee 100% accuracy on all information presented. This book is for educational and entertainment purposes only.

I make no representations about how much money you might make if you invest according to the criteria outlined in this book. Your personal returns will depend on the financial performance and dividend payouts of the individual stocks that you purchase. You are solely responsible for your individual investment decisions and the returns that you receive.

Nobody can predict the future. Past performance is no guarantee of future results.

I personally own a variety of dividend stocks including some of those mentioned in this book. As of the publishing of this book, I currently own shares of the following securities: AEP, APU, BFK, CMI, CMP, CXW, DUK, EMR, EPD, FAST, FLO, GE, GIS, GME, GPC, HCN, JNJ, KO, MMP, NLY, NZF, O, PAYX, PFF, PG, PM, SEP, SO, UPS, VTR, VZ and WFC. I am long on all of the securities that I own. Some of the companies I own have appreciated so much in the last few years that they have become overvalued and I would not buy them again today. I also own a few stocks that are short-term bets because I think they are currently oversold and the market has overreacted to negative news about them. It also possible that I have sold my stake some of my portfolio companies since this book was published.

While attempts have been made to verify information provided in this publication, neither the author nor the publisher assumes any responsibility for errors, omissions, or contrary interpretation of the subject matter herein. The publisher wants to stress that the information contained herein may be subject to varying state and/or local laws or regulations.

All readers are advised to retain competent counsel to determine what state and/or local laws or regulations may apply to the user's particular situation. The purchaser or reader of this publication assumes responsibility for the use of these materials and information. Adherence to all applicable laws and regulations, federal, state and local, governing professional licensing, operation practices, and all other aspects of operation in the US or any other jurisdiction is the sole responsibility of the purchaser or reader. The publisher and author assume no responsibility or liability whatsoever on the behalf of any purchaser or reader of these materials.

THANK YOU

THANK YOU FOR READING *Automatic Income* and choosing to spend some of your valuable time reading the information I have to offer. I hope that this book will inspire you to take action and build your own investment portfolio of dividend stocks.

If you would like to share your thanks for this book, the best thing you can do is tell a friend about *Automatic Income* or buy them a copy.

You can also show your appreciation for this book by leaving a review of the book on Amazon. To leave a review, visit the Amazon product page at www.AutomaticIncomeBook.com. Please be honest with your review and with how this book has or has not helped you on your journey to achieve your goal of launching your own Internet business. I want everyone to know if and/or how this book has changed your life in any significant way.

You can follow me online at my personal blog, MattPaulson.com. You can follow me on Twitter (@MatthewDP). You can follow me on Facebook at www.facebook.com/matthewpaulsonpage/. I am also on LinkedIn (linkedin.com/in/matthewpaulson) and AngelList (angel.co/matthewpaulson).

If you would like to hear me talk about various topics, feel free to check out the interviews I have done at mattpaulson.com/interviews.

Thank you and God bless,

Matthew Paulson
January 2017

ACKNOWLEDGMENTS

I **WOULD LIKE TO** express my sincere gratitude to my many friends, family members, and business acquaintances who have encouraged me while I have pursued various entrepreneurial adventures over the last decade.

I would like to thank my wife, Karine, for being incredibly supportive, putting up with my unusual work schedule, and trusting me to provide for our family through my business.

I would like to thank my children, Micah and Adylin, for the joy that they bring into my life.

I would like to thank my business partners and team members, including David Anicetti, Donna Helling, Todd Kolb, Don Miller, Tyler Prins, Rebecca McKeever, Jason Shea, Stevie Shea, and Toi Williams. Without them, my companies would not be where they are today.

Finally, I would like to express my gratitude to the many talented people who worked on this book.

I would like to thank Jennifer Harshman for editing this book and fixing my many grammar and spelling errors.

I would like to thank Rebecca McKeever for designing the cover of this book.

I would like to thank James Woosley for doing this book's layout.

I would like to thank Stu Gray for narrating the audio version of this book.

ABOUT THE AUTHOR

MATTHEW PAULSON IS THE founder of Market-
Beat.com, a financial media company committed to
making real-time investing information available to
investors at all levels. MarketBeat publishes a daily investment
newsletter to more than 425,000 subscribers and its network
of financial news websites attracts more than 4 million visi-
tors each month. MarketBeat's reporting has been covered by
a number of major financial media outlets, including Barron's
Magazine, the Wall Street Journal, CNBC, MarketWatch and
Seeking Alpha.

Through his books, his personal blog and his media appearances, Matthew teaches others about how to leverage the power of entrepreneurship in their lives and achieve personal financial freedom.

As an angel investor, Matthew has invested in a number of early-stage companies in a variety of verticals. He is also the chairman of Falls Angel Fund, a regional angel fund sponsored by the South Dakota Enterprise Institute has raised $1.3 million to invest in early-stage, high-growth companies in South Dakota and surrounding states.

Matthew holds a B.S. in Computer Science and an M.S. in Information Systems from Dakota State University. He also holds an M.A. in Christian Leadership from Sioux Falls Seminary.

Matthew resides in Sioux Falls, South Dakota, where he lives with his wife, Karine, and his two children, Micah and Adylin.

Connect with Matthew at:

- Matthew's Personal Blog: www.MattPaulson.com
- AngelList: www.angel.co/matthewpaulson
- Facebook: www.facebook.com/matthewpaulsonpage
- LinkedIn: www.LinkedIn.com/in/matthewpaulson
- Twitter: www.twitter.com/matthewdp
- Email: matt@mattpaulson.com

Other Books by Matthew Paulson

40 Rules for Internet Business Success:
Escape the 9 to 5, Do Work You Love
and Build a Profitable Online Business (2014)

Did you know that most "how to make money online" and "passive income" books are written by people that have never actually launched a real online business? Stop reading entrepreneurship books that were written by pretenders. Read *40 Rules for Internet Business Success* and you'll learn from a multi-millionaire entrepreneur that has created multiple six-figure and seven-figure online businesses from scratch.

Matthew Paulson, Founder of MarketBeat.com, has weathered the failures and triumphs of entrepreneurship for more than a decade. *40 Rules for Internet Business Success* is his collection of core principles and strategies he has used to identify new business ideas, launch new companies, and grow his businesses.

By reading *40 Rules for Internet Business Success*, you will learn to:

- Throw away your business plan! Create a scalable business model that actually works.
- Identify a target market that is desperate for your company's products and services.
- Launch your first product or service faster by building a minimum viable business.
- Create a reliable and repeatable marketing strategy to keep new customers coming.

- Understand why most "passive income" business ideas are doomed to fail (and how to beat the odds.)
- Build systems that make your business run like a well-oiled machine.
- Maximize your company's earnings potential with the three keys of revenue growth.

Whether you want to learn how to make money online, create passive income streams or build a massive online business empire, *40 Rules for Internet Business Success* will help you turn your dream of starting a business into reality.

Get Your Copy of *40 Rules for Internet Business Success* Here:

http://amzn.to/28Ooy8T

Email Marketing Demystified:
Build a Massive Mailing List, Write Copy that Converts and Generate More Sales (2015)

While many have decried that email is dead, a handful of digital marketers have quietly been using little-known email marketing techniques to generate massive results.

In *Email Marketing Demystified*, digital marketing expert Matthew Paulson reveals the strategies and techniques that top email marketers are currently using to build large mailing lists, write compelling copy that converts and generate millions in revenue using their email lists.

Inside the book, you'll learn how to:

- Build a massive mailing list using 15 different proven list building techniques.
- Write compelling copy that engages your readers and drives them to take action.
- Optimize every step of your email marketing funnel to skyrocket your sales.
- Grow a highly engaged and hungry fan base that will devour your content.
- Create six new revenue streams for your business using email marketing.
- Keep your messages out of the spam folder by following our best practices.

Matthew Paulson has organically grown an email list of more than 400,000 investors and generates more than $2 million per year in revenue using the strategies outlined in *Email Marketing Demystified*. Regardless of what kind of business you are building, email marketing can serve as the rocket fuel that that will skyrocket your business.

Get Your Copy of *Email Marketing Demystified* Here:

http://amzn.to/28XXqpJ

The Ten-Year Turnaround:

Transform Your Personal Finances and Achieve Financial Freedom in The Next Ten Years (2016)

Do you want to achieve financial freedom, but have no idea how to get there? Do you feel like you just aren't making enough money? Are your personal finances a mess? Are you stuck in debt and wish you could get out? Do you feel like your current financial plan isn't working or isn't working well enough?

If you said yes to any of these questions, it's time for you to begin your Ten-Year Turnaround. *The Ten-Year Turnaround* is a life-changing financial plan that will enable you to turn around your money problems and finally achieve financial freedom.

Here's what you'll learn:

- Grow your income by becoming an expert salary negotiator, starting your own business, or doing a side-hustle on nights and weekends.
- Become an expert money manager and avoid the most common mistakes that prevent people from building wealth.
- Build a dead-simple investment portfolio that will provide a lifetime stream of income.
- Learn proven wealth building techniques that allow anyone to grow their net worth, each and every month.

- Unlock the power of life-long learning and personal networking in your life so that career and business opportunities show up at your door.

- Reduce your taxes, prevent lawsuits, and eliminate financial risk from your life.

- Become a world-class philanthropist and learn how to effectively give money to charity.

In 2004, Matthew Paulson was a broke-and-in-debt college student who earned $7.00 an hour working at McDonalds. By using the personal finance and wealth-building strategies outlined in *The Ten-Year Turnaround*, Matthew was able to build a series of online businesses and amass a personal net worth of more than $10 million by the time he was thirty years old. Whether you're in debt or doing well, you can use the same personal finance strategies Matthew used to build wealth and achieve financial freedom faster than you ever thought possible.

Get Your Copy of *The Ten-Year Turnaround* Here:

http://amzn.to/28QNP4A

Business Growth Day by Day:

38 Lessons Every Entrepreneur Must Learn to Get More Done and Make More Money (2016)

Want to start or grow a business, but aren't getting any traction? Worried that you chose the wrong business idea? Entrepreneurship is a hard game to play, but it doesn't have to be as hard as many people make it out to be. Matthew Paulson outlines the business growth hacking and personal development shortcuts that multi-millionaires use to get ahead of the game in *Business Growth Day by Day.*

Whether you haven't made your first dollar yet or simply can't grow your business to the next level, there's one truth that every entrepreneur must learn:

Working harder isn't the answer.

Putting in enough hours usually isn't the problem. If you are like most entrepreneurs, you are already working harder than anyone else. What's really holding you back from building a successful business? If you're like many entrepreneurs, you're focusing on the wrong parts of your business. You're doing work your team members should be doing. You haven't paid enough attention to critical marketing tasks. You need to fine-tune your business model and pay closer attention to the books. *Business Growth Day by Day* reveals the commonly made, but little-known mistakes that almost every entrepreneur makes, which prevents them from achieving business success.

Here's What You'll Learn:

- The simple strategy that millionaires use to become smarter than everyone else.
- How to recognize and attract new business opportunities (and avoid the wrong ones).
- The single best way to make more money than you are today.
- Why using the word "no" might be the key to unlocking business growth.
- Why SEO, Google AdWords, and Facebook Ads might not be right for your business.
- The biggest small business mistakes commonly made by new entrepreneurs (and how to avoid them).
- How much your business ideas are actually worth—they may be less than you think.
- How your business can maintain an 80% profit margin, each and every month.
- How to effectively pitch your small business and yourself to others.
- When you should quit your day job and go full time with your business.
- What other business books aren't willing to tell you about entrepreneurship.
- Whether you should make a small business plan or just get started launching your business right away.

Matthew Paulson, Founder of MarketBeat.com, USGolfTV, and GoGo Photo Contest, has weathered the failures and triumphs of being an entrepreneur for more than a decade. He has built, grown, and sold multiple six-figure and seven-figure internet businesses using the strategies outlined in this book. Matthew believes that entrepreneurship is the single best way to help others and get what you want out of life. Through his business books, Matthew teaches others to create profitable businesses and achieve financial freedom.

Business Growth Day by Day has been referred to as "one of the must-read small business books to grow your company in 2016 and beyond." *Business Growth Day by Day* is chock-full of unique business ideas, plans, and strategies that will help you take your company to the next level.

Get Your Copy of *Business Growth Day by Day* Here:

http://amzn.to/29JViS7

Simple Savings:

274 Money-Saving Tips That Will Help You Save $1,000 or More Every Month (2016)

Are you tired of having too much month left at the end of your money? Do you feel like there's just never enough money to go around? Would having $100.00, $200.00, or $500.00 extra per month make a big difference in your life? Do you want to save money, but aren't sure where to start? If you can answer yes to any of these questions, *Simple Savings: 274 Money Saving Tips That Will Help You Save $1,000 or More Every Month* is the book for you.

Don't worry! This isn't another one of those books that tell you to pinch pennies and eat nothing but beans and rice. Rather, Simple Savings is chock-full of little-known, but highly effective money-saving strategies that will allow you to live the same lifestyle you are living today while leaving more money in your pocketbook. Authors Matthew Paulson and Toi Williams have collected hundreds of money-saving tips from savvy moms, frugal dads, and other smart shoppers and compiled them into an easy-to-read guide that will teach you to get more value out of each dollar you spend.

By reading *Simple Savings*, you will learn how to:

- Free up room in your budget so that you can spend more money on things that you actually enjoy.
- Reduce your family's grocery budget by $50.00 per week (while buying the same food you are today).

- Dramatically reduce the cost of your cable bill, your cell phone bill, and other nagging, recurring expenses.

- Cut the cost of transportation in half by spending less on gasoline and lowering your vehicle maintenance costs.

- Stop getting ripped off by your bank and get financial services that actually work for you (and not against you).

- Book a first-class trip on an economy budget using little-known travel hacks and other money-saving tips

Want to save money, live better, and spend less?

Saving money has never been easier when you read *Simple Savings: 274 Money Saving Tips That Will Help You Save $1,000 or More Every Month.*

Get your copy of *Simple Savings* and begin living larger on the money you already have.

Get Your Copy of *Simple Savings* Here:

http://www.amztk.com/simplesavings/

Online Business From Scratch
Your Internet Business Blueprint (2017)

Do you want to make money online? Are you tired of being told that it's easy to make millions off the Internet? Would you like a realistic strategy that actually works for real people? What if *you* could actually build an online business that offered high profit margins and required no significant up-front investment? Would you be interested?

It is possible to build your own profitable online business, but you can't do it overnight (despite what you have been told by so-called Internet-marketing gurus). The simple truth is that you need to choose a solid niche from day one, be willing to consistently work on your business over the course of several months, and follow the path laid before you by people who have actually done it.

This is not just another book by an "Internet marketing guru" that teaches you to "make money online."

Author Matthew Paulson has been building online businesses for more than a decade and he has built multiple six-figure and seven-figure Internet businesses in many different niches. He's not just another so-called "business guru" who makes money online by teaching people to make money online. His current company, MarketBeat.com, publishes an email newsletter to nearly 500,000 stock investors, attracts 3-5 million pageviews each month and generates more than $2.5 million in annual revenue each year. Matthew has also launched and sold a press-release distribution business, co-founded an online business that helps non-profits raise money, and is co-owner of a digital publishing company in the golf-instruction space.

By reading Matthew's book, *Online Business from Scratch*, you will receive his step-by-step plan that will show you exactly how to build your own profitable Internet business (even if you aren't very tech savvy).

Here's what you'll learn:

- Choose a niche that has strong advertiser demand, customers that are ready to buy, and solid long-term growth potential.

- Find the perfect domain name, create a great logo, and choose the ideal branding for your online business.

- Systematically build your audience through content marketing, social media marketing, paid advertising, and other audience-growth strategies.

- Develop a system that will make regularly creating great content a simple and straightforward process.

- Maximize your company's advertising revenue by choosing the right networks, setting up the right ad placements, and implementing other advanced monetization strategies.

- Launch digital products and services that your audience can't wait to buy.

- Position your business for long-term growth and establish systems so that your business can run without you.

Whether you simply want to learn how to make your first $1,000 online, create streams of passive income or build your own online business empire, *Online Business from Scratch* will help you turn your dream of starting an online business into reality.

Are you ready to take action?

Read *Online Business from Scratch* and begin your journey toward building your own online business today. Scroll to the top of the page and click on the buy button to get your copy of this book.

Get Your Copy of *Online Business from Scratch* here:

http://www.fromscratchbook.com

Made in the USA
Lexington, KY
27 September 2018